Learn Linux in 5 Days

JASON CANNON

JASON CANNON

Contents

OTHER BOOKS BY THE AUTHOR

Bash Command Line Pro Tips
http://www.linuxtrainingacademy.com/bash-pro-tips

Command Line Kung Fu: Bash Scripting Tricks, Linux Shell Programming Tips, and Bash One-liners
http://www.linuxtrainingacademy.com/command-line-kung-fu-book

High Availability for the LAMP Stack: Eliminate Single Points of Failure and Increase Uptime for Your Linux, Apache, MySQL, and PHP Based Web Applications
http://www.linuxtrainingacademy.com/ha-lamp-book

Python Programming for Beginners
http://www.linuxtrainingacademy.com/python-programming-for-beginners

YOUR FREE GIFT

As a thank you for reading *Learn Linux in 5 Days*, I would like to give you a copy of *Linux Alternatives to Windows Applications*. In it, you will be introduced to over 50 of the most popular applications available for Linux today. These applications will allow you to browse the web, watch movies, listen to music, connect to your favorite social networks, create presentations, and more. This gift is a perfect complement to this book and will help you along your Linux journey. Visit http://www.linuxtrainingacademy.com/linux-apps to download your free gift.

INTRODUCTION

As the founder of the Linux Training Academy and an instructor of several courses, I've had the good fortune of helping thousands of people hone their Linux skills. Interacting with so many people who are just getting started with the Linux operating system has given me invaluable insight into the particular struggles and challenges people face at this stage.

One of the biggest challenges for people interested in learning the ins and outs of Linux is simply a lack of time. When you are working with a limited and extremely valuable resource you want to make sure you make the most of it.

The next biggest challenge for Linux newcomers is knowing where to start. There is so much information available that deciding what to focus your attention on first is a big enough hurdle to keep many people from even starting. What's worse is starting down the path of learning only to discover too many concepts, commands, and nuances that aren't explained. This kind of experience is frustrating and leaves you with more questions than answers.

That's why I've written this book.

1

Not only have I condensed the most important material into five sections, each designed to be consumed in a day, I've also structured the content in a logical and systematic manner. This way you'll be sure to make the most out of your time by learning the foundational aspects of Linux first and then building upon that foundation each day.

In *Learn Linux in 5 Days* you will learn the most important concepts and commands, and be guided step-by-step through several practical and real-world examples. As new concepts, commands, or jargon are encountered they are explained in plain language, making it easy to understand.

Let's get started.

DAY 1

GETTING ACCESS

In order to start learning your way around and putting your newfound knowledge to the test, you're going to need access to a Linux system. If you already have an account on a Linux system, you can skip ahead to the next chapter.

Web Hosting Shell Accounts

If you use a web hosting service to host your website you may already have a Linux account that you can use. Consult your hosting company's documentation and search for "SSH" or "shell access." SSH stands for Secure Shell and it provides a way to connect to a server over a network, like the Internet. If you don't already have a web hosting provider, you can sign up for one and use it for shell access. Shared web hosting providers typically charge just a few dollars a month.

Here are some shared web hosting companies that can provide you with a shell account and SSH access.

- 1and1.com

- BlueHost.com

- DreamHost.com

- HostGator.com

- Site5.com

Using Preinstalled Linux Images

VirtualBox is virtualization software that can be installed on Windows, Mac, Solaris, or Linux. It allows you to run an operating system (guest) inside your current operating system (host). It's more time consuming than the other options, but it can be worth the extra effort to have your own personal Linux system. In this scenario you will spend a few minutes installing the virtualzation software, downloading a pre-installed Linux image, and importing that image.

To get started, head over to the VirtualBox download page located at https://www.virtualbox.org/wiki/Downloads and grab the installer for your current operating system. Click through the install screens and accept the defaults.

Next, download a virtual disk image (VDI) from http://virtualboxes.org to use. I recommend that you download a CentOS or Ubuntu image unless you already know which Linux distribution you will be working with in the future. Honestly, you can't make a wrong decision. The concepts that you will be learning in this book apply to any Linux distribution.

Launch VirtualBox, create a new virtual machine, and use the virtual disk image that you just downloaded. When you are asked for a hard disk image select the "Use existing hard disk" radio button and click on the directory icon. Next, click "Add" and select the virtual disk image.

When the virtual machine is powered on you can log into the server using the username and password provided with the downloaded image.

Deep Dive

These links along with other supplemental material is available at:

http://www.linuxtrainingacademy.com/lfb

- How to Install VirtualBox on Mac - A video that guides you through the installation of VirtualBox on Mac. http://youtu.be/xBQdflx1L1o

- How to Install VirtualBox on Windows - A video that guides you through the installation of VirtualBox on Windows. http://youtu.be/CBhppdewtEQ

- VirtualBox Documentation - Official VirtualBox documentation https://www.virtualbox.org/wiki/Documentation

- VirtualBox download page - Where to obtain a copy of the VirtualBox software. https://www.virtualbox.org/wiki/Downloads

- VirtualBoxes.org - A good source of virtual disk images. http://virtualboxes.org/

GETTING CONNECTED

When your account is created you will be provided with details on how to connect to the Linux server. You may be provided with some or all of the following information:

- Username. This is also known as an account, login, or ID.

- Password

- SSH key

- Server name or IP address

- Port number

- Connection protocol

The connection protocol will either be SSH (Secure Shell) or telnet. SSH and telnet provide ways to connect to a server over the Internet or a local area network. In the vast majority of cases the connection protocol will be SSH. Telnet is practically obsolete at this point, however you may run into it if you need to access a legacy system.

Choosing an SSH Client

If you were given a specific SSH client to use, use that program and follow the documentation for that product. If you are free to choose your own client or were not provided one, I suggest using PuTTY for Windows or Terminal for Mac.

PuTTY can be downloaded from this website: http://www.LinuxTrainingAcademy.com/putty/. You only need putty.exe to get started.

The Terminal application comes pre-installed on Macs and is located in the /Applications/Utilities folder.

A list of other SSH clients is provided in the Deep Dive section at the end of this chapter.

Connecting via SSH with a Password from Windows

To connect to the Linux server using the SSH connection protocol, launch PuTTY.

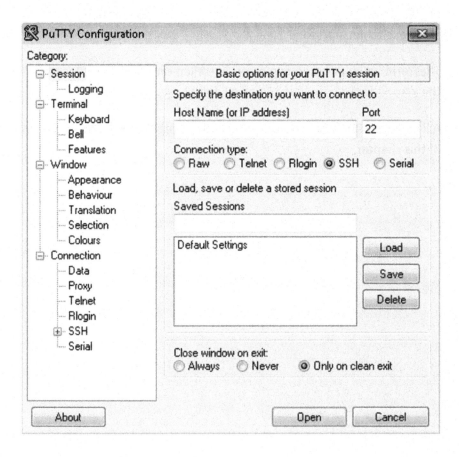

Type the host name or IP address you were given into the `Host Name (or IP address)` box. If no port was given to you, leave it at the default value of 22.

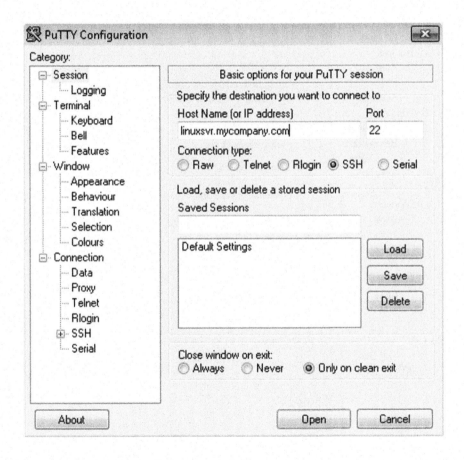

Enter your username by clicking on `Data` in the left pane. It is located directly below `Connection`. Type your username into the `Auto-login username` field. If you skip this step you will be prompted for your username when you connect to the server.

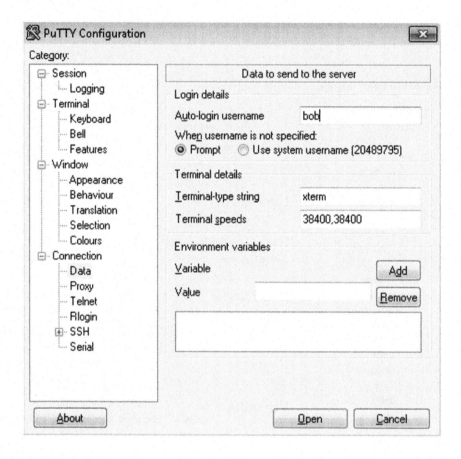

Save your session by typing in a name in the `Saved Sessions` box and clicking `Save`. This allows you to speed up this process by simply double clicking on your saved session to connect to the Linux server.

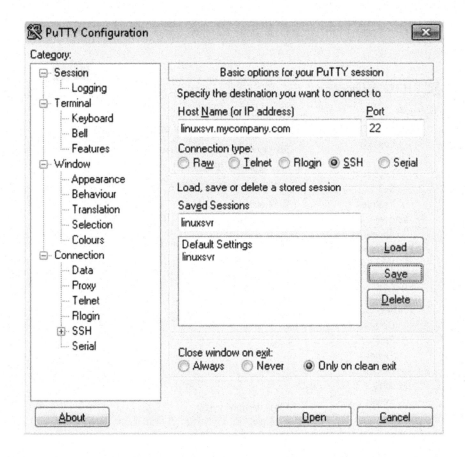

When you click `Open` a connection attempt will be made. The first time you connect to a particular server, PuTTY will ask to cache that server's host key. You will not be prompted again on subsequent connections. To add the server's SSH host key to PuTTY's cache, simply click `Yes` when prompted.

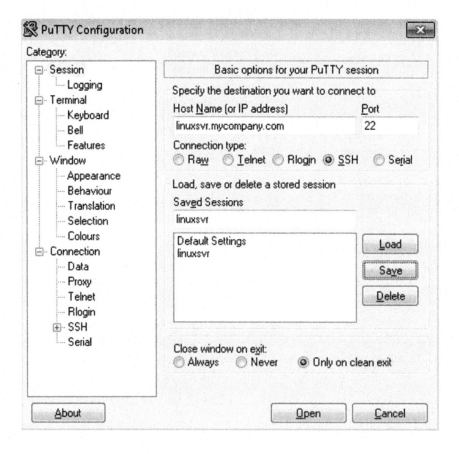

Once you are successfully logged in, you will see something similar to this:

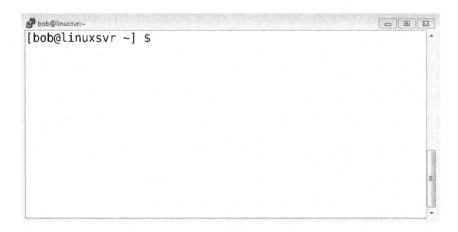

Connecting via SSH with a Password from Mac

The built-in SSH client on Mac is a command line program. Command line programs can be run with the `Terminal` application that comes with the Mac operating system. It is located in the `/Applications/Utilities` folder. The format of the ssh command is `ssh -p port_number username@servername`. If you were not provided a port number, then the default port of 22 is assumed and you can omit `-p 22` from the ssh command. Similarly, the username only needs to be specified if it is different on the server than it is on your Mac workstation. For example, if your username on your Mac is `bob` and your username on `linuxsvr` is also `bob`, you can omit `bob@` and simply type `ssh linuxsvr`. Once Terminal is running, type in the ssh command. Commands are case-sensitive and the `ssh` command is lowercase. It should look like one of these three options:

```
ssh linuxsvr
ssh bob@linuxsvr
ssh -p 2222 bob@linuxsvr
```

The first time you connect to a particular server you will be asked to verify that server's host key. You will not be prompted again on subsequent connections. When you are asked Are you sure you want to continue connecting (yes/no)? type yes and press Enter. Once you have established a connection, you will be prompted for your password.

Like Mac, Linux also comes with a terminal program and an SSH client. Once you are connected to one Linux server you can use the ssh command to connect to another Linux server. You can nest multiple connections and navigate through your network of Linux servers in this fashion.

General Information on Connecting via SSH with Keys

You may have not be given a password, but rather given an SSH key or even asked to generate one. In the physical world a key unlocks a door. Similarly, an SSH key is used to unlock the access to your account on a server. If you do not have a key, you cannot unlock the door.

Using account passwords or a combination of account passwords and SSH keys is a common practice. With the growth of cloud computing in recent years, it is becoming more and more popular to use SSH keys exclusively. Since cloud servers are often connected to the public internet, they are prone to brute force attacks. A mischievous person could write a program that repeatedly connects to your server trying a new username and password combination each time. They can increase their odds of gaining entry by using a list of common usernames and passwords. Configuring your cloud server to not accept account passwords and to only accept SSH keys eliminates this threat.

You can further increase the security of your SSH key by giving it a passphrase. In this case it takes something you have -- the key -- and something you know -- the passphrase -- to gain access to your account. If you feel confident that your key will only be under your control, you can forgo providing a passphrase for your key. This will allow you to log into servers without typing a password at all. Having an SSH key without a passphrase can allow you to automate and schedule tasks that require logging in to remote systems.

Importing SSH Keys on Windows

If you were given an SSH key that is not already in the PuTTY format, you will need to convert it. PuTTYgen is required in order to convert an SSH key on a Windows system.

17

Run PuTTYgen, click `Load` and navigate to the private SSH key you were given. The names of the files are typically id_rsa or id_dsa for private keys, and id_rsa.pub or id_dsa.pub for public keys.

Now you can save the public and private keys for later use with PuTTY.

Generating SSH Keys on Windows

In order to create an SSH key on a Windows system, you will need PuTTYgen.

When you run PuTTYgen you will be asked to move the mouse around to create some random data that will be used in the generation of the key.

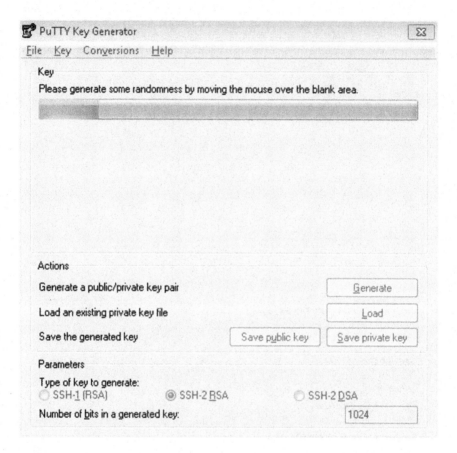

You have the option to use a passphrase for your key. You can also change the comment to something more meaningful like `Bob's key`.

Now, save the public and private keys buy pressing `Save public key` and then `Save private key`. Give the public key to the system administrator so they can associate it with your account. The private key is for your eyes only. Do not share your private key!

Next, export the key as an OpenSSH key by clicking on `Conversions` and then `Export OpenSSH Key`. This OpenSSH key can later be used on Unix or Linux systems.

Connecting via SSH from Windows

Follow the "Connecting via SSH with a Password from Windows" instructions, but this time add one additional step to specify your SSH private key file. You can do this by by clicking on the plug sign (+) next to `SSH` in the left pane to reveal more options. Next click on `Auth`. In the right pane select `Browse` under the `Private key file for authentication` field and locate your private SSH key.

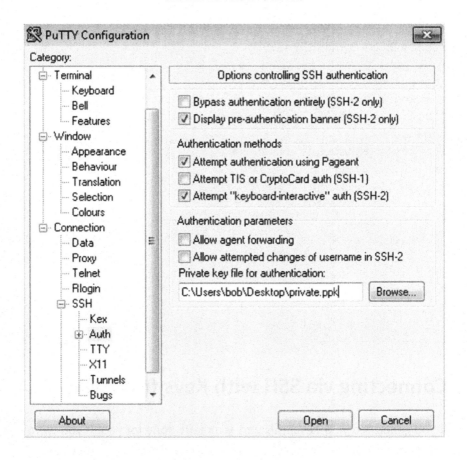

Generating SSH Keys on Mac

If you are asked to generate an SSH key, launch the Terminal application and use the command line utility named `ssh-keygen`. You will be asked a series of questions. Accept all the defaults by pressing `Enter`. Optionally enter a passphrase for your SSH key.

```
mac:~ bob$ ssh-keygen
Generating public/private rsa key pair.
Enter file in which to save the key
(/Users/bob/.ssh/id_rsa):
Enter passphrase (empty for no passphrase):
Enter same passphrase again:
```

```
Your identification has been saved in
/Users/bob/.ssh/id_rsa.
Your public key has been saved in
/Users/bob/.ssh/id_rsa.pub.
The key fingerprint is:
0b:14:c5:85:5f:55:77:35:5f:9e:15:a9:b4:b0:54:05
bob@mac
The key's randomart image is:
+--[ RSA 2048]----+
|        .o.o. .E+=@|
|       .o  o.. oO|
|     .  ...+ o.o|
|    .    .. o  |
|    . S        |
|    . .        |
|      .        |
|              |
|              |
+-----------------+
```

Connecting via SSH with Keys from Mac

If you generated your keys, this part is already done for you. If you were given an SSH key, you need to place it in a directory named .ssh underneath your home directory. Open the Terminal application and type in the following commands. Press the Enter key at the end of each line.

```
mkdir ~/.ssh
chmod 700 ~/.ssh
```

You will gain a full understanding of what these commands do as you progress through this book. In order to expedite the process of getting connected, the details will be saved for later.

Switch to the Finder to copy your keys into the .ssh folder. In the Finder menu click Go and then Go to Folder... and type ~/.ssh when prompted. When you click go, the .ssh folder will be displayed.

Now you can drag your keys into place.

```
                        Go to Folder

   Go to the folder:

   ~/.ssh

                              Cancel         Go
```

Back in the Terminal window, set the proper permissions on your key files. (Again, these commands will be covered later.)

```
cd ~/.ssh
chmod 600 *
```

I highly recommend naming the keys in the following format: id_rsa and id_rsa.pub or id_dsa and id_dsa.pub Otherwise, you will have to specify the location of your key when you use the ssh command or perform some additional configuration to tell SSH that your keys are not named in the standard way.

As a general rule it makes your life much easier if you follow the standard conventions and common practices. I will point them out along the way. One of the things I love most about Linux is the freedom and power it gives you to do things in a myriad of ways. There are cases where not following the standard conventions will be the right thing to do.

If you still wish to name your key something else, you can tell SSH where to find it by adding -i key_location to the ssh command. Remember, the format of the ssh command we used above is ssh -p

port_number username@servername. It can be expanded to
ssh   -i   key_location   -p   port_number
username@servername.   Here's   an   example:

```
ssh -i /Users/bob/.ssh/bobs_key bob@linuxsvr
```

Connecting via Telnet

Telnet used to be the de facto way to connect to a Unix or Linux server. Over the years telnet has been replaced with Secure Shell, abbreviated SSH. SSH is, as its name implies, more secure than telnet. Telnet sends your login credentials over the network in plain text. SSH encrypts the communications between the client and the server, thus greatly improving security. If someone were to be packet snooping or eavesdropping on your connection, they would see garbled text and random characters. If you do have a need to telnet to a system you can use the SSH instructions from above, but with a couple of minor changes.

Connecting via Telnet from Windows

Run PuTTY and select the `Telnet` radio button. If no port was given to you, leave it at the default value of 23. You will be prompted for your username and password when you connect to the server.

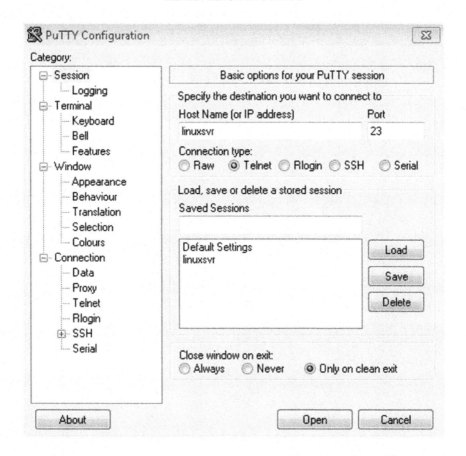

Connecting via Telnet from Mac

The built-in telnet client on Mac is a command line program. Command line programs can be run with the `Terminal` application that comes with the Mac operating system. It is located in the `/Applications/Utilities` folder. The format of the telnet command is `telnet servername port_number`. You only need to include a port number if it is different than the default value of 23. You will be prompted for your username and password when you connect to the server.

```
mac:~ bob$ telnet linuxsvr
Trying 10.0.0.7...
Connected to 10.0.0.7.
Escape character is '^]'.
Ubuntu 12.04.3 LTS
linuxsvr login: bob
Password:
Last login: Thu Nov  7 01:26:37 UTC 2013
Welcome to Ubuntu 12.04.3 LTS

 * Documentation:  https://help.ubuntu.com/

  System info as of Nov 7 01:26:52 UTC 2013

  System load:  0.42
  Usage of /:   3.1% of 40GB
  Memory usage: 32%
  Swap usage:   0%
  Processes:          89
  Users logged in:    0
  IP address for eth0: 10.0.0.7

bob@linuxsvr:~$
```

Connecting Directly

If you are running Linux in VirtualBox as described in the previous chapter or you have dedicated hardware with Linux installed on it, you can simply log in directly to the server. You will be presented with a prompt requesting your username and password. If it is a graphical environment, you will need to find a terminal application to use after you have logged in. In most cases it will literally be "terminal", but you might see some slight variations like "gnome terminal", "konsole", or "xterm."

Here is what opening the terminal application looks like in CentOS. You will find it in one of the menus.

28

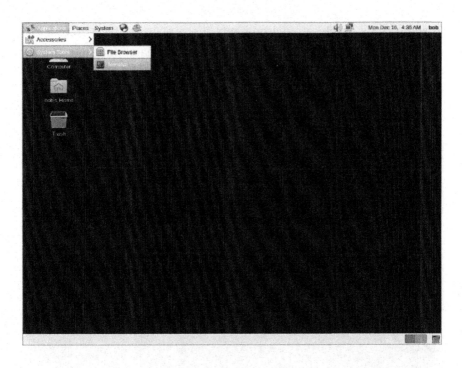

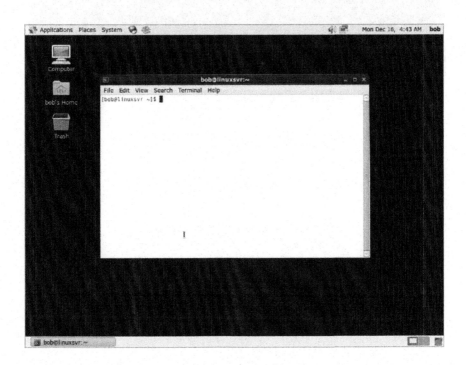

In some Linux graphical environments there may not be a traditional menuing system. In these cases you will want to search for the terminal application. In this Ubuntu example, click the button in the top left of the screen to bring up the dashboard. You can now start typing to find applications that are installed on the system.

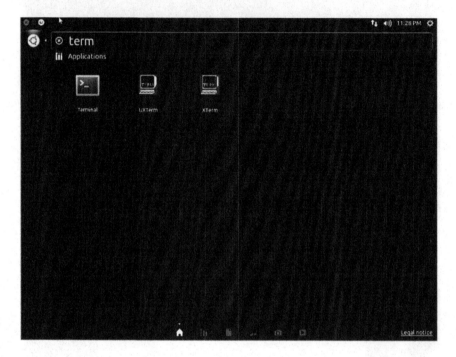

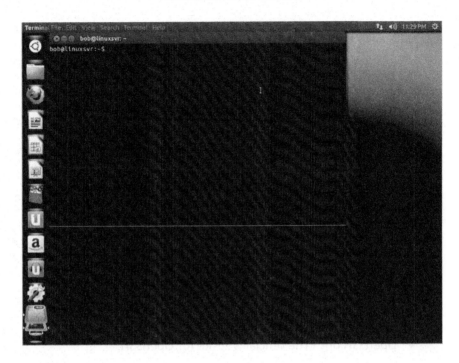

Deep Dive

- List of Mac SSH clients
  http://www.openssh.org/macos.html

- List of SSH clients, all platforms
  http://en.wikipedia.org/wiki/Comparison_of_SSH_clients

- List of Terminal Emulators - Includes terminals for
  Windows, Mac, and Linux.
  http://en.wikipedia.org/wiki/List_of_terminal_emulators

- List of Telnet Clients
  https://en.wikipedia.org/wiki/Telnet#Telnet_clients

- List of Windows SSH clients
  http://www.openssh.org/windows.html

- OpenSSH.org - The official website for OpenSSH.

- PuTTY
  http://www.LinuxTrainingAcademy.com/putty/

- Watch Star Wars over a telnet connection.

    - `telnet towel.blinkenlights.nl`

    - To disconnect, hold down the `Ctrl` key and
      press the right bracket (`]`). At the `telnet >`
      prompt type `quit` and press `Enter`.

- Using SSH Public Key Authentication
  http://macnugget.org/projects/publickeys

WELCOME TO SHELL

When you log into a server over the network the shell program is started and acts as your default interface to the system. The shell is nothing more than a program that accepts your commands and executes those commands. Said another way, the shell is a command line interpreter.

Let's look at the shell prompt you'll be working with. The prompt just sits and stares at you waiting for you do something interesting like give it a command to execute. Here is Bob's shell prompt.

```
bob@linuxsvr $
```

Bob's prompt is in a common format of `username@servername $`. In this example, the prompt is displaying the username, the server name, and if that user is using the system as a normal user ($) or a superuser (#).

The superuser on a Linux system is also called root. Anything that can be done on a server can be done by root. However, normal users can only do a subset of the things root can do. Root access is typically restricted to system administrators, but if you happen to support an application on a Linux server you may need root privileges to install, start, or stop it. There are ways to grant specific users root privileges for specific cases. This is often accomplished with the sudo -- SuperUser Do -- program. That will be covered later. For now, just know that most of your day to day activities will be performed using a normal user account.

Your prompt might not look like Bob's. Common items that appear in prompts include the username, server name, present working directory, and the current time. Here are a few more prompt examples.

```
[bob@linuxsvr /tmp]$
linuxsvr:/home/bob>
bob@linuxsvr:~>
[16:45:51 linuxsvr ~]$
$
%
>
```

In two of the prompt examples you will notice a tilde (~). The tilde is a shorthand way of representing your home directory. In this example the tilde (~) is equivalent to /home/bob, which is Bob's home directory. This is called tilde expansion. A username can be specified after the tilde and it will be expanded to the given user's home directory. For example, ~mail would expand to the home directory of the mail user which is /var/spool/mail. Another example is ~pat expanding to /home/pat.

Prompts do not have to be contained on a single line. They can span multiple lines as in the following examples.

```
linuxsvr:[/home/bob]
$

(bob@linuxsvr)-(06:22pm-:-11/18)-]-
(~)

[Mon 13/11/18 18:22 EST][pts/0][x86_64]
<bob@linuxsvr:~>
```

```
zsh 14 %
```

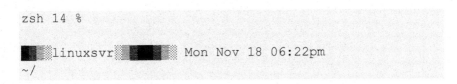

```
~/
```

For the remainder of this book the prompt will be shortened to the dollar sign ($) unless displaying the full prompt provides additional clarity. Also, the default prompt may vary from system to system, but you can customize it to your liking. That, along with other shell related topics, is covered in a later chapter.

Deep Dive

- Tilde Expasion
  http://gnu.org/software/bash/manual/html_node/Tilde-Expansion.html

DAY 2

LINUX DIRECTORY STRUCTURE

Now that you are able to connect to the server and have been introduced to the interface you will be using, it's time to learn about the directory layout. Understanding the directory structure will help you in the future when you are searching for components on the system. It can help you answer questions like:

Where are programs located?

Where do configuration files live?

Where might I find the log files for this application?

Common Directories

Here are the most common top level directories that you need to be aware of and may interact with as a normal user.

Dir	Description
/	The directory called "root." It is the starting point for the file system hierarchy. Note that this is not related to the root, or superuser, account.
/bin	Binaries and other executable programs.
/etc	System configuration files.
/home	Home directories.
/opt	Optional or third party software.
/tmp	Temporary space, typically cleared on reboot.
/usr	User related programs.
/var	Variable data, most notably log files.

Comprehensive Directory Listing

Here is a comprehensive list of top level directories that you may find on various Linux systems. Some subdirectories are included to help clearly define the purpose of the top level directory. You may never interact with many of these directories. Some of these directories will be on every system you encounter like /usr. Other directories are unique to specific Linux distributions. You can safely skim over this list and refer back to it if or when you have a practical need to do so.

Dir	Description
/	The directory called "root." It is the starting point for the file system hierarchy. Note that this is not related to the root, or superuser, account.
/bin	Binaries and other executable programs.
/boot	Files needed to boot the operating system.
/cdrom	Mount point for CD-ROMs.
/cgroup	Control Groups hierarchy.
/dev	Device files, typically controlled by the operating system and the system administrators.
/etc	System configuration files.
/export	Shared file systems. Most commonly found on Solaris systems.
/home	Home directories.
/lib	System Libraries.
/lib64	System Libraries, 64 bit.
/lost+found	Used by the file system to store recovered files after a file system check has been performed.
/media	Used to mount removable media like CD-ROMs.
/mnt	Used to mount external file systems.
/opt	Optional or third party software.

Dir	Description
/proc	Provides information about running processes.
/root	The home directory for the root account.
/sbin	System administration binaries.
/selinux	Used to display information about SELinux.
/srv	Contains data which is served by the system.
/srv/www	Web server files.
/srv/ftp	FTP files.
/sys	Used to display and sometimes configure the devices and busses known to the Linux kernel.
/tmp	Temporary space, typically cleared on reboot. This directory can be used by the OS and users alike.
/usr	User related programs, libraries, and documentation. The sub-directories in /usr relate to those described above and below.
/usr/bin	Binaries and other executable programs.
/usr/lib	Libraries.
/usr/local	Locally installed software that is not part of the base operating system.
/usr/sbin	System administration binaries.
/var	Variable data, most notably log files.

Dir	Description
`/var/log`	Log files.

Unix Specific Directories

Linux is often found in environments with other Unix variants. If you ever have a need to log into a Unix server you may see some of the following Unix specific directories.

Dir	Description
`/devices`	Device files, typically controlled by the operating system and the system administrators.
`/kernel`	Kernel and kernel modules. (Solaris)
`/platform`	Platform specific files. (Solaris)
`/rpool`	ZFS root pool directory. (Solaris)
`/net`	Used to mount external file systems. (HP-UX)
`/nfs4`	Used to mount the Federated File System domain root. (Solaris)
`/stand`	Files needed to boot HP-UX.

Note that you may encounter other top level directories that have not been listed above. However, those were most likely created by the system administrator.

Application Directory Structures

Applications can follow the same conventions employed by the operating system. Here is a sample directory structure of an application named `apache` installed in `/usr/local`.

Dir	Description
`/usr/local/apache/bin`	The application's binaries and other executable programs.
`/usr/local/apache/etc`	Configuration files for the application.
`/usr/local/apache/lib`	Application libraries.
`/usr/local/apache/logs`	Application log files.

Here is what it might look like if it was installed in `/opt`.

Dir	Description
`/opt/apache/bin`	The application's binaries and other executable programs.
`/opt/apache/etc`	Configuration files for the application.
`/opt/apache/lib`	Application libraries.
`/opt/apache/logs`	Application log files.

A common alternative to placing all the application subdirectories in `/opt/app-name` is to also use `/etc/opt/app-name` and `/var/opt/app-name`. Here is what that might look like for our example `apache` application.

Dir	Description
/etc/opt/apache	Configuration files for the application.
/opt/apache/bin	The application's binaries and other executable programs.
/opt/apache/lib	Application libraries.
/var/opt/apache	Application log files.

Sometimes applications that are not part of the standard operating system are installed in a shared manner and are not given their own subdirectory. For example, if apache was installed directly into /usr/local its binaries would live in /usr/local/bin and its configuration would live in /usr/local/etc. Apache may not be the only locally installed software so it would share that space with the other installed applications.

Another common practice is to create a directory structure based on a company, organization, or team name. For example, if you work at the Acme Corporation you may find a directory named /opt/acme or /usr/local/acme. Sometimes scripts and utilities are installed directly in that structure and other times there are segregated into their own subdirectories. Here's an example.

Dir	Description
/opt/acme	Company top level directory.
/opt/acme/bin	Binary programs created by or installed by the Acme Corporation.

Alternatively you may see something like this.

Dir	Description
/opt/acme	Company top level directory.
/opt/acme/apache	The top level directory for Acme's installation of apache.
/opt/acme/apache/bin	The apache binary programs.

Here are variations on the same idea, but based on a team within the company.

Dir	Description
/opt/web-team	The web support team's top level directory.
/opt/acme/web-team	The web support team's top level directory.
/usr/local/acme/web-team	The web support team's top level directory.

Example Top Level Directory Listings

Here is a listing of the top level directories for a few different Linux servers. Listing files and directories with the ls command will be covered in the next chapter.

Red Hat Enterprise Linux 7 (RHEL)

```
[bob@rhel6 ~]$ ls -1 /
bin
boot
cgroup
dev
etc
home
lib
lib64
lost+found
media
mnt
opt
proc
root
sbin
selinux
srv
sys
tmp
usr
var
```

SUSE Linux Enterprise Server 11 (SLES)

```
[bob@sles11 ~]$ ls -1 /
bin
boot
dev
etc
home
lib
lib64
lost+found
media
mnt
opt
proc
root
```

```
sbin
selinux
srv
sys
tmp
usr
```

Ubuntu 14.04 LTS

```
[bob@ubuntu12 ~]$ ls -1 /
bin
boot
dev
etc
home
lib
lib64
lost+found
media
mnt
opt
proc
root
run
sbin
selinux
srv
sys
tmp
usr
var
```

Deep Dive

- Filesystem Hierarchy Standard
  http://refspecs.linuxfoundation.org/FHS_2.3

- man hier

- RedHat Enterprise Linux
  http://redhat.com/products/enterprise-linux/

- SUSE Linux Enterprise Server
  https://www.suse.com/products/server/

- Ubuntu
  http://www.ubuntu.com/

BASIC LINUX COMMANDS

Here is a short list of basic, but essential commands. In Linux, commands are case-sensitive and more often than not they are entirely in lowercase. Items that are surrounded by brackets ([]) are optional. You will more than likely use at least some of these commands every time you log into a Linux system. Become familiar with these commands because they can get you pretty far in a short amount of time.

ls - Lists directory contents. You will use ls to display information about files and directories.

cd [dir] - Changes the current directory to dir. If you execute cd without specifying a directory, cd changes the current directory to your home directory. This is how you navigate around the system.

pwd - Displays the present working directory name. If you don't know what directory you are in, pwd will tell you.

cat [file] - Concatenates and displays files. This is the command you run to view the contents of a file.

echo [argument] - Displays arguments to the screen.

man command - Displays the online manual for command. Type q to quit viewing the manual page. The documentation provided by the man command is commonly called "man pages."

exit, logout, or Ctrl-d - Exits the shell or your current session.

clear - Clears the screen.

Here is a screen capture of Bob's session using the above commands.

```
$ ls
PerformanceReviews sales-lecture.mp3 sales.data
tpsreports
$ cd tpsreports
$ pwd
/home/bob/tpsreports
$ ls -l
total 2
-rw-r--r-- 1 bob users 31 Sep 28 14:49 coversheet.doc
-rw-r--r-- 1 bob users 35 Sep 27 08:47 sales-report
$ cat sales-report
We sold lots of widgets this week!
$ echo $PATH
/bin:/usr/bin:/usr/sbin:/usr/local/bin
$ man ls
NAME
       ls - list directory contents
...
```

More details on how you can fully exploit the power of these simple commands will be covered later. But right now, grab your fishing pole -- you're about to learn how to fish.

TEACH YOURSELF TO FISH

Knowing where executable commands live and the man command can take you a long way. You can teach yourself how to use Linux with this method, but it would be a long, slow process. More often than not, the man command will be used as a quick reference. It would be nearly impossible to memorize every option for every command and there is no need to do so when you have the man command at your fingertips.

To get help for the man command type the letter h while viewing a manual page. That will give you a list of commands you can use to navigate or search. Here is the concise version.

Enter - Move down one line.

Space - Move down one page.

g - Move to the top of the page.

G - Move to the bottom of the page.

q - Quit.

An environment variable is a storage location that has a name and a value. The one we are interested in at the moment is PATH. The PATH environment variable contains a list of directories that contain executable commands. You can determine the value of PATH by prepending it with a dollar sign ($PATH) and using the echo command to display its value to the screen.

```
$ echo $PATH
/bin:/usr/bin:/usr/sbin:/usr/local/bin
```

When you type in a command at the prompt and press Enter, that command will be searched for in the directories in your $PATH. In this example, /bin will be searched first. If the command is found it will be executed. If it is not found, then /usr/bin will be searched and so on. If no executable command is found that matches your request, you will be politely told that it cannot be found.

```
$ whatsupdoc
-bash: whatsupdoc: command not found
```

If you want to know exactly where a command is located you can use the which command. If the program cat is located in /usr/bin and in /usr/local/bin, the one which will get executed depends on your $PATH.

```
$ which cat
/bin/cat
$ which tac
/usr/bin/tac
```

Putting this all together, you can start looking at what is in each directory in your $PATH and use the man command to discover what each one of them does and how to use them. Remember, to exit the man command type the letter q.

```
$ echo $PATH
/bin:/usr/bin:/usr/sbin:/usr/local/bin
$ cd /bin
$ ls
awk diff cal cat cp date du echo grep groups less
```

```
more
$ man diff
NAME
      diff - compare two files
...
$ cd /usr/bin
$ ls
clear crontab cut dos2unix find kill mv pstree pwd
sed strings touch ...
$ man touch
```

Note that the output of the above `ls` commands was truncated. In reality there can be hundreds of commands in /bin and /usr/bin.

Many commands will provide hints for how to use them at the command line. Some commands will accept the `-h` flag, others will accept `--help`, and some will refuse to give you any help at all.

```
$ cal -h

Usage:
 cal [options] [[[day] month] year]

Options:
 -1, --one       show only current month (default)
 -3, --three     show previous, current and next month
 -s, --sunday    Sunday as first day of week
 -m, --monday    Monday as first day of week
 -j, --julian    output Julian dates
 -y, --year      show whole current year
 -V, --version   display version information and exit
 -h, --help      display this help text and exit
$ diff --help
Usage: diff [OPTION]... FILES
Compare files line by line.

  -i --ignore-case  Ignore case differences in file
contents.
  --ignore-file-name-case  Ignore case when comparing
file names.
```

. . .

If you are not sure what command to use, you can search through the man pages with man -k KEYWORD. From there you can read the man page for the command or ask it for help with -h or --help.

```
$ man -k calendar
cal          (1)  - display a calendar
zshcalsys    (1)  - zsh calendar system
```

Deep Dive

- ExplainShell - Type in a command-line to display help for each item.
  http://explainshell.com/

- Getting Help From Linux - An article from the Linux Journal on using man pages.
  http://www.linuxjournal.com/node/1022962

- LinuxManPages.com - This website allows you to search man pages or browse a category of commands and man pages.
  http://www.linuxmanpages.com/

- Linux commands broken down by category.
  http://linux.math.tifr.res.in/manuals/categories-index.html

WORKING WITH DIRECTORIES

Directories are simply containers for files and other directories. They provide a tree like structure for organizing the system. Directories can be accessed by their name and they can also be accessed using a couple of shortcuts. Linux uses the symbols . and .. to represent directories. Think of . as "this directory" and .. and "the parent directory."

Symbol	Description
.	This directory.
..	The parent directory.
/	Directory separator. Directories end in a forward slash and this is often assumed.

The directory separator is optional for the last subdirectory in a path or command. For example, the following commands work identically.

```
$ cd /var/tmp
$ cd /var/tmp/
```

Using the shortcuts can make navigating easier. For example, type cd.. to go to the directory just above your current directory.

```
$ pwd
/home/bob
$ cd tpsreports
$ pwd
/home/bob/tpsreports
$ cd ..
$ pwd
/home/bob
$ cd ..
$ pwd
/home
$ cd .
$ pwd
/home
```

The cd . command did not take you anywhere. Remember that . is "this directory" and .. is "the parent directory." Another shortcut for navigating directories is cd -. This command takes you to the previous directory. The environment variable that represents your previous working directory is OLDPWD. So, cd - and cd $OLDPWD are equivalent.

```
$ pwd
/home/bob
$ cd /var/tmp
$ pwd
/var/tmp
$ echo $OLDPWD
/home/bob
$ cd -
/home/bob
$
```

How would you execute a command that is in your current directory? Assume your current directory is your home directory. By default your home directory is not in your $PATH. Here is how to do that.

```
$ ./program
```

Why does that work? Well, . represents "this directory", / is the directory separator, and program is the program to execute. You can always use the full path to be explicit. Here are two ways to execute program.

```
$ pwd
/home/bob
$ ./program
$ /home/bob/program
```

Creating and Removing Directories

The mkdir command is used to create directories and the rmdir command removes them.

mkdir [-p] directory - Create a directory. Use the -p (parents) option to create intermediate directories.

rmdir [-p] directory - Remove a directory. Use the -p (parents) option to remove all the specified directories. rmdir only removes empty directories. To remove directories and their contents, use rm.

rm -rf directory - Recursively removes the directory and all files and directories in that directory structure. *Use with caution.* There is no "trash" container to quickly restore your file from when using the command line. When you delete something, it is gone.

```
$ mkdir newdir
$ mkdir newdir/product/reviews
mkdir: Failed to make directory
"newdir/product/reviews"; No such file or directory
$ mkdir -p newdir/product/reviews
$ rmdir newdir
rmdir: directory "newdir": Directory not empty
$ rm -rf newdir
$ ls newdir
ls: newdir: No such file or directory
$ pwd
/home/bob
$ cd ..
$ pwd
/home
```

LISTING FILES AND UNDERSTANDING LS OUTPUT

Here is the output from an `ls` command using the `-l` option. The `-l` flag tells `ls` to display output in a long format. If you need to see what files or directories exist, use `ls`. However, if you need detailed information use `ls -l`.

```
$ ls -l
-rw-rw-r-- 1 bob users 10400 Sep 27 08:52 sales.data
```

On the far left of the `ls` output is a series of characters that represent the file permissions. The number that follows the permissions represents the number of links to the file. The next bit of information is the owner of the file followed by the group name. Next the file size is displayed followed by the date and time when the file was last modified. Finally, the name of the file or directory is displayed. Here is the information displayed by the `ls -l` command in table form.

Item	Value
Permissions	-rw-rw-r--
Number of links	1

Item	Value
Owner name	bob
Group name	users
Number of bytes in the file	10400
Last modification time	Sep 27 08:52
File name	sales.data

The meaning of `-rw-rw-r--` will be covered in detailed in the "File and Directory Permissions Explained" chapter.

Listing All Files, Including Hidden Files

Files or directories that begin with a period (.) are considered hidden and are not displayed by default. To show these hidden files and directories, use the `-a` option.

```
$ ls -a
.
..
.profile
.bash_history
lecture.mp3
PerfReviews
sales.data
tpsreports
```

Up until this point when you have used options, you have preceded each option with a hyphen (-). Examples are `-l` and `-a`. Options that do not take arguments can be combined. Only one hyphen is required followed by the options. If you want to show a long `ls` listing with hidden files you could run `ls -l -a` or `ls -la`. You can even change the order of the flags, so `ls -al` works too. They are all equivalent.

```
$ ls -l
total 2525
-rw-r--r--  1  bob   sales   25628  Sep 27 08:54 lecture.mp3
drwxr-xr-x  3  bob   users   512    Sep 28 09:20 PerfReviews
-rw-r--r--  1  bob   users   10400  Sep 27 08:52 sales.data
drwxr-xr-x  2  bob   users   512    Sep 28 14:49 tpsreports
$ ls -l -a
total 2532
drwxr-xr-x  4  bob   sales   512    Sep 28 14:56 .
drwxr-xr-x  14 root  root    512    Sep 27 08:43 ..
-rw-r--r--  1  bob   users   28     Sep 28 14:22 .profile
-rw-------  1  bob   users   3314   Sep 28 14:56 .bash_history
-rw-r--r--  1  bob   sales   25628  Sep 27 08:54 lecture.mp3
drwxr-xr-x  3  bob   users   512    Sep 28 09:20 PerfReviews
-rw-r--r--  1  bob   users   10400  Sep 27 08:52 sales.data
drwxr-xr-x  2  bob   users   512    Sep 28 14:49 tpsreports
$ ls -la
total 2532
drwxr-xr-x  4  bob   sales   512      Sep 28 14:56 .
drwxr-xr-x  14 root  root    512      Sep 27 08:43 ..
-rw-r--r--  1  bob   users   28       Sep 28 14:22 .profile
-rw-------  1  bob   users   3314     Sep 28 14:56
.bash_history
-rw-r--r--  1  bob   sales   25628  Sep 27 08:54 lecture.mp3
drwxr-xr-x  3  bob   users   512    Sep 28 09:20 PerfReviews
-rw-r--r--  1  bob   users   10400  Sep 27 08:52 sales.data
drwxr-xr-x  2  bob   users   512    Sep 28 14:49 tpsreports
$ ls -al
total 2532
drwxr-xr-x  4  bob   sales   512    Sep 28 14:56 .
drwxr-xr-x  14 root  root    512    Sep 27 08:43 ..
-rw-r--r--  1  bob   users   28     Sep 28 14:22 .profile
-rw-------  1  bob   users   3314   Sep 28 14:56 .bash_history
-rw-r--r--  1  bob   sales   25628  Sep 27 08:54 lecture.mp3
drwxr-xr-x  3  bob   users   512    Sep 28 09:20 PerfReviews
-rw-r--r--  1  bob   users   10400  Sep 27 08:52 sales.data
drwxr-xr-x  2  bob   users   512    Sep 28 14:49 tpsreports
```

Listing Files by Type

When you use the -F option for ls a character is appended to the file name that reveals what type it is.

```
$ ls
dir1 link program regFile
$ ls -F
dir1/ link@ program* regFile
$ ls -lF
total 8
drwxr-xr-x 2 bob users 117 Sep 28 15:31 dir1/
lrwxrwxrwx 1 bob users 7   Sep 28 15:32 link@ -> regFile
-rwxr-xr-x 1 bob users 10  Sep 28 15:31 program*
-rw-r--r-- 1 bob users 750 Sep 28 15:32 regFile
```

Symbol	Meaning
/	Directory.
@	Link. The file that follows the -> symbol is the target of the link.
*	Executable program.

A link is sometimes called a symlink, short for symbolic link. A link points to the location of the actual file or directory. You can operate on the link as if it were the actual file or directory. Symbolic links can be used to create shortcuts to long directory names. Another common use is to have a symlink point to the latest version of installed software as in this example.

```
bob@linuxsvr:~$ cd /opt/apache
bob@linuxsvr:/opt/apache ~$ ls -F
2.3/ 2.4/ current@
bob@linuxsvr:/opt/apache$ ls -l
drwxr-xr-x 2 root root 4096 Sep 14 12:21 2.3
drwxr-xr-x 2 root root 4096 Nov 27 15:43 2.4
lrwxrwxrwx 1 root root    5 Nov 27 15:43 current -> 2.4
```

Listing Files by Time and in Reverse Order

If you would like to sort the ls listing by time, use the -t option.

```
$ ls -t
tpsreports
PerfReviews
lecture.mp3
sales.data
$ ls -lt
total 2532
drwxr-xr-x 2 bob users 512      Sep 28 14:49 tpsreports
drwxr-xr-x 3 bob users 512      Sep 28 09:20 PerfReviews
-rw-r--r-- 1 bob sales 2562856  Sep 27 08:54 lecture.mp3
-rw-r--r-- 1 bob users 10400    Sep 27 08:52 sales.data
```

When you have a directory that contains many files it can be convenient to sort them by time, but in reverse order. This will put the latest modified files at the end of the `ls` output. The old files will scroll off the top of your display, but the most recent files will be right above your prompt.

```
$ ls -latr
total 2532
drwxr-xr-x 14 root root 512     Sep 27 08:43 ..
-rw-r--r-- 1 bob users 10400    Sep 27 08:52 sales.data
-rw-r--r-- 1 bob sales 256285   Sep 27 08:54 lecture.mp3
drwxr-xr-x 3 bob users 512      Sep 28 09:20 PerfReviews
-rw-r--r-- 1 bob users 28       Sep 28 14:22 .profile
drwxr-xr-x 2 bob users 512      Sep 28 14:49 tpsreports
drwxr-xr-x 4 bob sales 512      Sep 28 14:56 .
-rw------- 1 bob users 3340     Sep 28 15:04 .bash_history
```

Listing Files Recursively

Using the -R option with `ls` causes files and directories to be displayed recursively.

```
$ ls -R
.:
PerfReviews lecture.mp3 sales.data tpsreports
./PerfReviews:

Fred John old

./PerfReviews/old:
Jane.doc
$
```

You can also use the `tree` command for more visually appealing output. If you only want to see the directory structure, use `tree -d`.

`tree` - List contents of directories in a tree-like format.

`tree -d` - List directories only.

`tree -C` - Colorize output.

```
$ tree
.
├── PerfReviews
│   ├── Fred
│   ├── John
│   └── old
│       └── Jane.doc
├── sales.data
├── sales-lecture.mp3
└── tpsreports

2 directories, 6 files
$ tree -d
.
└── PerfReviews
    └── old

2 directories
$
```

List Directories, Not Contents

Normally when you run `ls` against a directory the contents of that directory are displayed. If you want to ensure you only get the directory name, use the −d option.

```
$ ls -l PerfReviews
total 3
-rw-r--r-- 1 bob users  36 Sep 27 08:49 Fred
-rw-r--r-- 1 bob users  36 Sep 28 09:21 John
drwxr-xr-x 2 bob users 512 Sep 27 12:40 old
$ ls -ld PerfReviews
drwxr-xr-x 3 bob users 512 Sep 28 09:20 PerfReviews
$ ls -d PerfReviews
PerfReviews
```

Listing Files with Color

Earlier you used `ls -F` to help differentiate file types by adding a character to the end of their names in the `ls` output. You can also use color to distinguish file types by using `ls --color`.

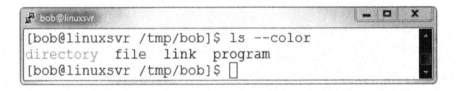

```
[bob@linuxsvr /tmp/bob]$ ls --color
directory  file  link  program
[bob@linuxsvr /tmp/bob]$ []
```

Commonly Used `ls` Options

Here is a recap of the `ls` options you have learned.

Option	Description
`-a`	All files, including hidden files
`--color`	List files with colorized output
`-d`	List directory names and not their contents
`-l`	Long format
`-r`	Reverse order
`-R`	List files recursively
`-t`	Sort by time, most recently modified first

Working with Spaces in Names

If you want to make your life easier when working from the command line, do not use spaces in file and directory names. Hyphens (-) or underscores (_) can be good substitutes for spaces. CamelCase, the practice of capitalizing each word, is another good option. For example, instead of naming your latest literary attempt "the next great american novel.txt" you could use "the-next-great-american-novel.txt", "the_next_great_american_novel.txt" or even "TheNextGreatAmericanNovel.txt."

Sooner or later you will encounter a file or directory that contains a space in the name. There are two ways to deal with this. The first is to use quotation marks. Even though the file name is `a file`, operate on it using `"a file."` The second option is to escape the space. Escaping is like using quotes, but for single characters. The escape symbol is \, also known as a backslash. To escape a space, precede the space with the backslash (\) character.

```
$ ls -l
-rw-r--r-- 1 bob users 18 Oct 2 05:03 a file
$ ls -l a file
ls: a: No such file or directory
ls: file: No such file or directory
$ ls -l "a file"
-rw-r--r-- 1 bob users 18 Oct 2 05:03 a file
$ ls -l a\ file
-rw-r--r-- 1 bob users 18 Oct 2 05:03 a file
$ ls -lb a*
-rw-r--r-- 1 bob users 18 Oct 2 05:03 a\ file
$
```

The −b option to ls causes it to print escape codes. Note that quoting and escaping not only applies to spaces, but with other special characters as well including | & ' ; ( ) < > space tab.

Deep Dive

- Escaping Special Characters in Linux and Unix: With 7 Practical Examples - An article that takes a in-depth look at escaping. http://linuxg.net/escaping-special-characters-in-linux-and-unix-with-7-practical-examples/

- man bash - Look at the "QUOTING" section for handling special characters including spaces.

- man ls - To learn about all of the available options to ls refer to the man page.

DAY 3

FILE AND DIRECTORY PERMISSIONS EXPLAINED

Looking back at the long listings provided by the `ls` command you see that the first bit of information displayed is the permissions for the given file or directory.

```
$ ls -l sales.data
-rw-r--r-- 1 bob users 10400 Sep 27 08:52 sales.data
```

The first character in the permissions string reveals the type. For example, – is a regular file, `d` is a directory, and `l` is a symbolic link. Those are the most common types you will encounter. For a full listing read the `ls` man page.

Symbol	Type
–	Regular file
d	Directory
l	Symbolic link

You will also notice other characters in the permissions string. They represent the three main types of permissions which are read, write, and execute. Each one is represented by a single letter, also known as a symbol. Read is represented by r, write by w, and execute by x.

Symbol	Permission
r	Read
w	Write
x	Execute

Read, write, and execute are rather self explanatory. If you have read permissions you can see the contents of the file. If you have write permissions you can modify the file. If you have execute permissions you can run the file as a program. However, when these permissions are applied to directories they have a slightly different meaning than when they are applied to files.

Permission	File Meaning	Directory Meaning
Read	Allows a file to be read.	Allows file names in the directory to be read.
Write	Allows a file to be modified.	Allows entries to be modified within the directory.
Execute	Allows the execution of a file.	Allows access to contents and metadata for entries in the directory.

There are three categories of users that these permissions can be applied to. These categories or classes are user, group, and other. Like the permission types, each set is represented by a single letter. The user who owns the file is represented by u, the users that are in the file's group are represented by g, and the other users who do not own the file or are not in the file's group are represented by o. The character a represents all, meaning user, group, and other. Even though these characters do not show up in an ls listing, they can be used to change permissions.

Symbol	Category
u	User
g	Group
o	Other
a	All - user, group, and other.

Every user is a member of at least one group called their primary group. However, users can and often are members of many groups. Groups are used to organize users into logical sets. For example, if members of the sales team need access to some of the same files and directories they can be placed into the sales group.

Run the groups command to see what groups you are a member of. If you supply another users ID as an argument to the groups command you will see the list of groups to which that user belongs. You can also run id -Gn [user] to get the same result.

```
$ groups
users sales
$ id -Gn
users sales

$ groups pat
users projectx apache
$ groups jill
users sales manager
```

Secret Decoder Ring for Permissions

Now you have enough background information to start decoding the permissions string. The first character is the type. The next three characters represent the permissions available to the user, also known as the owner of the file. The next three characters represent the permissions available to the members of the file's group. The final three characters represent the permissions available to all others.

In this case order has meaning. Permission types will be displayed for user, followed by group, and finally for others. Also, the permission types of read, write, and execute are displayed in that order. If a particular permission is not granted a hyphen (–) will take its place.

Here is a graphical representation of the permission information displayed by `ls -l`.

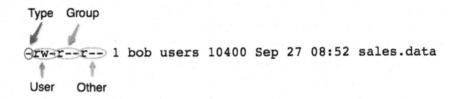

```
-rw-r--r-- 1 bob users 10400 Sep 27 08:52 sales.data
```

If you happen to see an extra character at the end of the permissions string an alternative access control method has been applied. If you see a period (.), the file or directory has an SELinux (Security Enhanced Linux) security context applied to it. If you see a plus sign (+), ACLs (Access Control Lists) are in use. SELinux and ACLs are beyond the scope of this book. However, you will be pleased to know that the use of either of these is rare. If you are having troubles with permissions and notice an extra character in the permissions string, know that further investigation may be necessary.

```
$ ls -l sales.data.selnx
-rw-r--r--. 1 bob users 1040 Sep 27 08:52 sales.data.selnx
$ ls -l sales.data.acl
-rw-r--r--+ 1 bob users 1040 Sep 27 08:52 sales.data.acl
```

Changing Permissions

Permissions are also known as modes. That is why the command you use to change permissions is called chmod, short for "change mode." The format of the chmod command is chmod mode file. There are two ways to specify the mode. The first way is called symbolic mode. The symbolic mode format is chmod user_category operator permission. Here is a table view of the chmod command symbolic mode format.

Item	Meaning
chmod	The change mode command.
ugoa	The user category. One or more of u for user, g for group, o for other, a for all.
+-=	One of +, −, or =. Use + to add permissions, − to subtract them, or = to explicitly set them.
rwx	The permissions. One or more of r for read, w for write, and x for execute.

You can add, subtract, or set permissions using user category and permission pairs. For example, if you want to add the write permission for the members of a file's group, you would specify chmod g+w file.

```
$ ls -l sales.data
-rw-r--r-- 1 bob users 10400 Sep 27 08:52 sales.data
$ chmod g+w sales.data
$ ls -l sales.data
-rw-rw-r-- 1 bob users 10400 Sep 27 08:52 sales.data
```

Notice that after running chmod g+w sales.data the permissions string changed from '-rw-r--r--' to '-rw-rw-r--'. Remember that the permissions are displayed in the order of user, group, and other. The group permission set now includes the w symbol indicating that the write permission has been granted. Now the owner of the file (bob) and members of the group (users) can read and write to the sales.data file. Here is the reverse. This is how you would subtract the write permission.

```
$ ls -l sales.data
-rw-rw-r-- 1 bob users 10400 Sep 27 08:52 sales.data
$ chmod g-w sales.data
$ ls -l sales.data
-rw-r--r-- 1 bob users 10400 Sep 27 08:52 sales.data
```

You can change more than one permission at a time. This time write and execute permissions are added for the file's group.

```
$ ls -l sales.data
-rw-r--r-- 1 bob users 10400 Sep 27 08:52 sales.data
$ chmod g+wx sales.data
$ ls -l sales.data
-rw-rwxr-- 1 bob users 10400 Sep 27 08:52 sales.data
```

You can even set permissions on different user categories simultaneously. Here is how to change permissions for the user and group. Notice that before running this command that the user already has the write permissions. Using + to add permissions does not negate any existing permissions, it just adds to them.

```
$ ls -l sales.data
-rw-r--r-- 1 bob users 10400 Sep 27 08:52 sales.data
$ chmod ug+wx sales.data
$ ls -l sales.data
-rwxrwxr-- 1 bob users 10400 Sep 27 08:52 sales.data
```

If you want to set different permissions for different user categories, you can separate the specifications with a comma. You can mix and match to produce the outcome you desire. Here is how you can specify `rwx` for user while adding `x` for group.

```
$ ls -l sales.data
-rw-r--r-- 1 bob users 10400 Sep 27 08:52 sales.data
$ chmod u=rwx,g+x sales.data
$ ls -l sales.data
-rwxr-xr-- 1 bob users 10400 Sep 27 08:52 sales.data
```

If you want to set the file to be just readable by everyone, run `chmod` `a=r file`. When you use the equal sign (=) the permission are set to exactly what you specify. If you specify just read, then only read will be available regardless of any existing permissions.

```
$ ls -l sales.data
-rw-r--r-- 1 bob users 10400 Sep 27 08:52 sales.data
$ chmod a=r sales.data
$ ls -l sales.data
-r--r--r-- 1 bob users 10400 Sep 27 08:52 sales.data
```

If you do not specify permissions following the equal sign, the permissions are removed. Here is an illustration of this behaviour

```
$ ls -l sales.data
-rw-r--r-- 1 bob users 10400 Sep 27 08:52 sales.data
$ chmod u=rwx,g=rx,o= sales.data
$ ls -l sales.data
-rwxr-x--- 1 bob users 10400 Sep 27 08:52 sales.data
```

Numeric Based Permissions

In addition to symbolic mode, octal mode can be used with `chmod` to set file and directory permissions. Understanding the concepts behind symbolic mode will help you learn octal mode. However, once you learn octal mode you may find that it is even quicker and easier to use than symbolic mode. Since there are only a few common and practical permission modes they can be readily memorized and recalled.

In octal mode permissions are based in binary. Each permission type is treated as a bit that is either set to off (0) or on (1). In permissions, order has meaning. Permissions are always in read, write, and execute order. If r, w, and x are all set to off, the binary representation is 000. If they are all set to on, the binary representation is 111. To represent read and execute permissions while omitting write permissions, the binary number is 101.

r	w	x	
0	0	0	Binary Value for off
1	1	1	Binary Value for on
r	w	w	
0	0	0	Base 10 (decimal) value for off
4	2	1	Base 10 (decimal) value for on

To get a number that can be used with chmod, convert the binary representation into base 10 (decimal). The shortcut here is to remember that read equals 4, write equals 2, and execute equals 1. The permissions number is determined by adding up the values for each permission type. There are eight possible values from zero to seven, hence the name octal mode. This table demonstrates all eight of the possible permutations.

Octal	Binary	String	Description
0	000	---	No permissions
1	001	--x	Execute only
2	010	-w-	Write only
3	011	-wx	Write and execute (2 + 1)
4	100	r--	Read only
5	101	r-x	Read and execute (4 + 1)
6	110	rw-	Read and write (4 + 2)
7	111	rwx	Read, write, and execute (4+2+1)

Again, in permissions order has meaning. The user categories are always in user, group, and other order. Once you determine the octal value for each category you specify them in that order. For example, to get -rwxr-xr--, run chmod 754 file. That means the user (owner) of the file has read, write, and execute permission; the members of the file's group have read and execute permission; and others have read permissions

	U	G	O
Symbolic	rwx	r-x	r--
Binary	111	101	100
Decimal	7	5	4

Commonly Used Permissions

Here are the most commonly used permissions. These five permissions will let you do just about anything you need to permissions wise.

Symbolic	Octal	Use Case / Meaning
-rwx------	700	Ensures a file can only be read, edited, and executed by the owner. No others on the system have access.
-rwxr-xr-x	755	Allows everyone on the system to execute the file but only the owner can edit it.
-rw-rw-r--	664	Allows a group of people to modify the file and let others read it.
-rw-rw----	660	Allows a group of people to modify the file and not let others read it.
-rw-r--r--	644	Allows everyone on the system to read the file but only the owner can edit it.

When you encounter 777 or 666 permissions, ask yourself "Is there a better way to do this?" "Does everybody on the system need write access to this?" For example, if a script or program is set to 777, then anyone on the system can make changes to that script or program. Since the execute bit is set for everyone, that program can then be executed by anyone on system. If malicious code was inserted either on purpose or on accident it could cause unnecessary trouble. If multiple people need write access to a file consider using groups and limiting the access of others. It is good practice to avoid using 777 and 666 permission modes.

Working with Groups

If you work on the sales team and each member needs to update the sales.report file, you would set the group to sales using the chgrp command and then set the permissions to 664 (rw-rw-r--). You could even use 660 (rw-rw----) permissions if you want to make sure only members of the sales team can read the report. Technically 774 (rwxrwxr--) or 770 (rwxrwx---) permissions work also, but since sales.report is not an executable program it makes more sense to use 664 (rw-rw-r--) or 660 (rw-rw----).

When you create a file its group is set to your primary group. This behaviour can be overridden by using the newgrp command, but just keep in mind when you create a file it typically inherits your default group. In the following example Bob's primary group is users. Note that the format of the chgrp command is chgrp GROUP FILE.

```
$ nano sales.report
$ ls -l sales.report
-rw-r--r-- 1 bob users 6 Dec  4 20:41 sales.report
$ chgrp sales sales.report
$ ls -l sales.report
-rw-r--r-- 1 bob sales 6 Dec  4 20:41 sales.report
$ chmod 664 sales.report
$ ls -l sales.report
-rw-rw-r-- 1 bob sales 6 Dec  4 20:41 sales.report
```

Instead of keeping files in the home directories of various team members, it is easier to keep them in a location dedicated to the team. For example, you could ask the system administrator of the server to create a /usr/local/sales directory. The group should be set to sales and the permissions should be set to 775 (rwxrwxr-x) or 770 (rwxrwx---). Use 770 (rwxrwx---) if no one outside the sales team needs access to any files, directories, or programs located in /usr/local/sales.

```
$ ls -ld /usr/local/sales
drwxrwxr-x 2 root sales 4096 Dec  4 20:53
/usr/local/sales
$ mv sales.report /usr/local/sales/
$ ls -l /usr/local/sales
total 4
-rw-rw-r-- 1 bob sales 6 Dec  4 20:41 sales.report
```

Directory Permissions Revisited

This example demonstrates how permissions effect directories and their contents. A common problem is having proper permissions set on a file within a directory only to have the incorrect permissions on the directory itself. Not having the correct permissions on a directory can prevent the execution of the file, for example. If you are sure a file's permissions have been set correctly, look at the parent directory. Work your way towards the root of the directory tree by running ls -ld . in the current directory, moving up to the parent directory with cd .., and repeating those two steps until you find the problem.

```
$ ls -dl directory/
drwxr-xr-x 2 bob users 4096 Sep 29 22:02 directory/
$ ls -l directory/
total 0
-rwxr--r-- 1 bob users    0 Sep 29 22:02 testprog
$ chmod 400 directory
$ ls -dl directory/
dr-------- 2 bob users 4096 Sep 29 22:02 directory/
$ ls -l directory/
ls: cannot access directory/testprog: Permission
denied
total 0
-????????? ? ? ? ?            ? testprog
$ directory/testprog
-su: directory/testprog: Permission denied
$ chmod 500 directory/
$ ls -dl directory/
dr-x------ 2 bob users 4096 Sep 29 22:02 directory/
```

```
$ ls -l directory/
total 0
-rwxr--r-- 1 bob users 0    Sep 29 22:02 testprog
$ directory/testprog
This program ran successfully.
```

Default Permissions and the File Creation Mask

The file creation mask is what determines the permissions a file will be assigned upon its creation. The mask restricts or masks permissions, thus determining the ultimate permission a file or directory will be given. If no mask were present directories would be created with 777 (rwxrwxrwx) permissions and files would be created with 666 (rw-rw-rw-) permissions. The mask can and is typically set by the system administrator, but it can be overridden on a per account basis by including a umask statement in your personal initialization files.

umask [-S] [mode] - Sets the file creation mask to mode if specified. If mode is omitted, the current mode will be displayed. Using the -S argument allows umask to display or set the mode with symbolic notation.

The mode supplied to umask works in the opposite way as the mode given to chmod. When you supply 7 to chmod, that is interpreted to mean all permissions on or rwx. When you supply 7 to umask, that is interpreted to mean all permissions off or ---. Think of chmod as turning on, adding, or giving permissions. Think of umask as turning off, subtracting, or taking away permissions.

A quick way to estimate what a umask mode will do to the default permissions is to subtract the octal umask mode from 777 in the case of directories and 666 in the case of files. Here is an example of a umask 022 which is typically the default umask used by Linux distributions or set by system administrators.

```
                   Dir    File
Base Permission    777    666
Minus Umask       -022   -022
                  ----   ----
Creation Permission 755    644
```

Using a umask of 002 is ideal for working with members of your group. You will see that when files or directories are created the permissions allow members of the group to manipulate those files and directories.

```
                   Dir    File
Base Permission    777    666
Minus Umask       -002   -002
                  ----   ----
Creation Permission 775    664
```

Here is another possible umask to use for working with members of your group. Use 007 so that no permissions are granted to users outside of the group.

```
                   Dir    File
Base Permission    777    666
Minus Umask       -007   -007
                  ----   ----
Creation Permission 770    660 *
```

Again, using this octal subtraction method is a good estimation. You can see that the method breaks down with the umask mode of 007. In reality, to get an accurate result each time you need to convert the octal permissions into binary values. From there you use a bitwise NOT operation on the umask mode and then perform a bitwise AND operation against that and the base permissions.

It is fine to gloss over the subtleties here since there are only a few practical umask modes to use. They are 022, 002, 077, and 007. Save yourself the binary math homework and look at the following table containing all the resulting permissions created by each one of the eight mask permutations.

Octal	Binary	Dir Perms	File Perms
0	000	rwx	rw-
1	001	rw-	rw-
2	010	r-x	r--
3	011	r--	r--
4	100	-wx	-w-
5	101	-w-	-w-
6	110	--x	---
7	111	---	---

Special Modes

Look at this output of umask when the mask is set to 022.

```
$ umask
0022
```

You will notice an extra leading 0. So far you have only been dealing with three characters that represent permissions for user, group, and other. There is a class of special modes. These modes are setuid, setgid, and sticky. Know that these special modes are declared by prepending a character to the octal mode that you normally use with umask or chmod. The important point here is to know that umask 0022 is the same as umask 022. Also, chmod 644 is the same as chmod 0644.

Even though special modes will not be covered in this book, here they are for your reference. There are links at the end of this chapter so you can learn more about these modes if you are so inclined.

setuid permission - Allows a process to run as the owner of the file, not the user executing it.

setgid permission - Allows a process to run with the group of the file, not of the group of the user executing it.

sticky bit - Prevents a user from deleting another user's files even if they would normally have permission to do so.

umask Examples

Here are two examples of the effects umask modes have on file and directory creation.

```
$ umask
0022
$ umask -S
u=rwx,g=rx,o=rx
$ mkdir a-dir
$ touch a-file
$ ls -l
total 4
drwxr-xr-x 2 bob users 4096 Dec  5 00:03 a-dir
-rw-r--r-- 1 bob users    0 Dec  5 00:03 a-file
$ rmdir a-dir
$ rm a-file
$ umask 007
$ umask
0007
$ umask -S
u=rwx,g=rwx,o=
$ mkdir a-dir
$ touch a-file
$ ls -l
total 4
drwxrwx--- 2 bob users 4096 Dec  5 00:04 a-dir
-rw-rw---- 1 bob users    0 Dec  5 00:04 a-file
```

Free Training Videos on Linux Permissions

I know learning Linux permissions can be challenging. That's why I've recorded two videos that cover this subject in depth. In the videos I not only explain the concepts behind Linux permissions, but I also demonstrate them on an actual Linux server. Watching these will reinforce what you've learned in this chapter and hopefully clear up any confusion you might have. You can watch them here: http://www.linuxtrainingacademy.com/perms/

Deep Dive

- Binary Number System - There are only 10 kinds of people in the world: those who understand binary and those who don't.
http://mathsisfun.com/binary-number-system.html

- Every Possible Umask Mode - An article that lists every possible umask mode.
http://linuxtrainingacademy.com/all-umasks

- Linux Permissions Explained Videos
Watch these two videos that explain and demonstrate Linux file system permissions.
http://www.linuxtrainingacademy.com/perms/

- Modes - Detailed permission information.
https://en.wikipedia.org/wiki/Modes_(Unix)

- SELinux - The official SELinux project page.
http://selinuxproject.org/

- Special File Permissions - An article describing setuid, setgid, and the sticky bit.
http://docs.oracle.com/cd/E19683-01/806-4078/secfiles-69

- Ubuntu ACL Documentation – This applies not only to Ubuntu, but to other Linux distributions as well.
http://help.ubuntu.com/community/FilePermissionsACLs

FINDING FILES

If you ever need to locate a file or directory you can use the `find` command. It can be used to find files by name, size, permissions, owner, modification time, and more.

`find [path...] [expression]` - Recursively finds files in path that match expression. If no arguments are supplied it find all files in the current directory.

```
$ find
.
./.profile
./.bash_history
./PerfReviews
./PerfReviews/Fred
./PerfReviews/current
./PerfReviews/current/tps-violations.log
./PerfReviews/John
./sales.data
...
```

Here are some useful ways in which to use the `find` command.

`find . -name pattern` - Displays files whose name matches pattern. This is case sensitive.

`find . -iname pattern` - Same as –name, but ignores case.

`find . -ls` - Performs an ls on each of the found files or directories.

`find . -mtime num_days` - Finds files that are num_days old.

`find . -size num` - Finds files that are of size num.

`find . -newer file` - Finds files that are newer than file.

`find . -exec command {} \;` - Run command against all the files that are found.

Let's look at some examples. Let's say you are looking for a file or directory named "apache." You think it is in /opt somewhere and are not quite sure if it is "Apache" or "apache." You could provide `find` with the path of /opt, use `-iname` to ignore case, and look for "apache."

```
$ find /opt -iname apache
/opt/web/Apache
```

To find all the files in /usr/local that end in "conf", you can use this command.

```
$ find /usr/local -name *conf
/usr/local/etc/dhcpd.conf
/usr/local/etc/httpd.conf
```

If you are looking for files that are more than 10 days old, but less than 13 days old in the current directory you can use this command.

```
$ find . -mtime +10 -mtime -13
././.profile
./PerfReviews
```

```
./PerfReviews/John
./tpsreports
./tpsreports/coversheet.doc
```

Find files that start with an "s" and perform an `ls` on them.

```
$ find . -name "s*" -ls
52  11 -rw-r--r-- 1 bob users 1040 Sep 27 08:52 ./sales.data
48   1 -rw-r--r-- 1 bob users   35 Sep 27 08:47 ./demos/sr.txt
53 112 -rw-r--r-- 1 bob sales  266 Sep 27 08:54 ./salesdemo.mp3
```

The `-size` argument to `find` takes a number followed by a letter that represents the unit of space. Valid options are:

c for bytes

k for Kilobytes (units of 1024 bytes)

M for Megabytes (units of 1048576 bytes)

G for Gigabytes (units of 1073741824 bytes)

Here is an example of how to find files that are larger than 300 megabytes.

```
$ find . -size +300M
./PerfReviews/current/tps-violations.log
```

Here is how to find directories that are newer than a given file. In this case you are looking for directories that are newer that "b.txt."

```
$ find . -type d -newer b.txt
./PerfReviews
./PerfReviews/current
./tpsreports
```

On some occasions you may want to run a command against a list of files. You can use the `find` command with the `-exec` option to do this sort of thing. Use a pair of braces (`{}`) to act as a placeholder for the current file being processed. The command is terminated with the semicolon (;) character. You need to either escape or quote the semicolon like this ';' or like this \;. If you want to run the command file FILE_NAME on every file in the current directory you would use the following command.

```
$ find . -exec file {} \;
.: directory
./.profile: ASCII text
./.bash_history: ASCII text
./PerfReviews: directory
./PerfReviews/Fred: directory
./PerfReviews/current: directory
./PerfReviews/current/tps-violations.log: ASCII text
./PerformanceReviews/John: empty
./sales.data: data
```

As you can see find is a really powerful tool and it has even more features than you have seen so far. Take a look at the man page or refer to the links at this end of this chapter.

Locate - A fast find

Every time you run the find command it evaluates each file and returns the appropriate response. This can be a slow process at times. For instance, if you are looking for a file on the system and cannot narrow its location down to a subdirectory you would run find / - name something. That command looks at each and every file on the system. If you know the file's name or at least part of its name and just want to know where it resides, the locate command is the right tool for that job.

locate pattern - List files that match pattern.

Once a day all the files on the system are indexed by a process called updatedb. When you run locate it is simply querying the index or database created by updatedb and not looking at each file on the system. This is really, really fast. The down side is that the data is not in real time. If you are trying to find a file you created just a few minutes ago, chances are it is not yet indexed and `locate` will not find it. Also, `locate` can potentially return a file that matches your search, but the file may have removed from the system since the index was last updated. On some servers `locate` is not installed or enabled, so your only choice may be to use `find`.

Here is what it looks like when `locate` is disabled.

```
$ locate bob
locate: /var/locatedb: No such file or directory
```

If it is enabled you will get a quick response to your queries. Notice that you do not need to know the entire file name, just a portion works.

```
$ locate tpsrep
/home/bob/tpsreports
/home/bob/tpsreports/coversheet.doc
/home/bob/tpsreports/sales-report.txt
```

Deep Dive

- Find - Ubuntu documentation on the find command.
  https://help.ubuntu.com/community/find

- Locate - An article on the locate command.
  http://www.linfo.org/locate.html

- The /etc/passwd file - An article on the `/etc/passwd` file.
  http://www.linfo.org/etc_passwd.html

VIEWING AND EDITING FILES

Here are some simple commands that display the contents of files to the screen.

`cat file` - Display the entire contents of file.

`more file` - Browse through a text file. Press the `Spacebar` to advance to the next page. Press `Enter` to advance to the next line. Type `q` to quit viewing the file. Commands are based on the `vi` editor, which is covered in the next section.

`less file` - Like more but allows backward movement and pattern searches.

`head file` - Output the beginning (or top) portion of file.

`tail file` - Output the ending (or bottom) portion of file.

This is how you might examine a file named `file.txt` with the commands `cat`, `tail`, and `more`.

```
$ cat file.txt
This is the first line.
This is the second.
Here is some more interesting text.
Knock knock.
Who's there?
More filler text.
The quick brown fox jumps over the lazy dog.
The dog was rather impressed.
Roses are red,
Violets are blue,
All my base are belong to you.
Finally, the 12th and last line.
$ head file.txt
This is the first line.
This is the second.
Here is some more interesting text.
Knock knock.
Who's there?
More filler text.
The quick brown fox jumps over the lazy dog.
The dog was rather impressed.
Roses are red,
Violets are blue,
$ tail file.txt
Here is some more interesting text.
Knock knock.
Who's there?
More filler text.
The quick brown fox jumps over the lazy dog.
The dog was rather impressed.
Roses are red,
Violets are blue,
All my base are belong to you.
Finally, the 12th and last line.
$ more file.txt
Here is some more interesting text.
Knock knock.
Who's there?
...
```

By default head and tail only display ten lines. You can override this behavior and tell them to display a specified number of lines. The format is -n where n is the number of lines you want to display. If you only want to display the first line of a file use head -1 file. Want to display the last three lines? Then run tail -3 file.

```
$ head -2 file.txt
This is the first line.
This is the second.
$ tail -1 file.txt
Finally, the 12th and last line.
$
```

Viewing Files In Real Time

Using cat can be a fine way to view files that have fairly static content. However, if you are trying to keep up with changes that are being made in real time to a file, cat is not the best choice. A good example of files that can change often and rapidly are log files. For example, you may need to start a program and look at that program's log file to see what it is doing. For this case, use the tail -f file command.

tail -f file - Follow the file. Displays data as it is being written to the file.

```
$ tail -f /opt/app/var/log.txt
Oct 10 16:41:17 app: [ID 107833 user.info] Processing
request 7680687
Oct 10 16:42:28 app: [ID 107833 user.err] User pat
denied access to admin functions
. . .
```

Editing Files

Nano

If you need to edit a file right now and do not want to spend any time learning obscure editor commands, use nano. Nano is a clone of pico, so if for some reason the nano command is not available, pico probably is. It's not as powerful as some other editors, but it's definitely easier to learn.

When you start nano you will see the file's contents and a list of commands at the bottom of the screen. To run the commands, replace the caret symbol (^) with the Ctrl key. For example, to exit nano type Ctrl-x.

Editing in nano is quite easy. The up and down arrow keys will take you to the previous or next lines as expected. The right and left arrow keys let you navigate forwards and backwards on the same line. Simply type the desired text into the editor. To save the file, type Ctrl-o. If you forget to save the file before you exit, nano will ask you if you want to save the file. To learn more type Ctrl-g for help.

Vi

While nano is great for simple edits, vi and emacs have more advanced and powerful features. There is a learning curve to using these editors as they are not exactly intuitive. It will require a bit of a time investment to become proficient. Let's start by looking at vi.

vi [file] - Edit file.

vim [file] - Same as vi, but with more features.

view [file] - Starts vim in read-only mode. Use view when you want to examine a file but not make any changes.

Vim stands for "Vi IMproved." It is compatible with the commands found in vi. Some of the additional features of vim include syntax highlighting, the ability to edit files over the network, multi-level undo/redo, and screen splitting. On many Linux distributions when you invoke vi, you are actually running vim.

One advantage of knowing vi is that vi or a vi variant like vim is always available on the system. Another advantage is that once you learn the key mappings for vi you can apply them to other commands like man, more, less, view, and even your shell.

Vi Modes

Command Mode

Vi has the concept of modes. You are always working in one of three modes: command mode, insert mode, or line mode. When vi starts you are placed into command mode. To get back to command mode at any time hit the escape key (Esc). Letters typed while in command mode are not sent to the file, but are rather interpreted as commands. Command mode allows you to navigate about the file, perform searches, delete text, copy text, and paste text.

Here are some commonly used key bindings for navigation.

k - Up one line.

j - Down one line.

h - Left one character.

l - Right one character.

w - Right one word.

b - Left one word.

^ - Go to the beginning of the line.

$ - Go to the end of the line.

Note that commands are case sensitive. For example, if you want to move down one line type the lowercase j. The uppercase J joins lines together. The original vi editor did not employ the use of arrow keys, however vim does, so you may find that you can use arrow keys on your system. The advantages of learning the original key bindings are 1) they always work and 2) it's faster since your hand does not have to leave the home row.

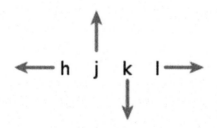

Insert mode

To enter insert mode, press one of the following keys.

i - Insert at the cursor position.

I - Insert at the beginning of the line.

a - Append after the cursor position.

A - Append at the end of the line.

After entering into insert mode, type the desired text. When you are finished, type Esc to return to command mode.

Line mode

To enter line mode you must start from command mode and then type a colon (:) character. If you are in insert mode, type Esc to get back to command mode and then type a colon for line mode. Here are some of the most common line mode commands you will want to know.

:w - Writes (saves) the file.

:w! - Forces the file to be saved even if the write permission is not set. This only works on files you own.

:q - Quit. This will only works if there have not been any modifications to the file.

:q! - Quit without saving changes made to the file.

:wq! - Write and quit. After modifying a file this command ensures it gets saved and closes vi.

:x - Same as :wq.

:n - Positions the cursor at line n. For example, :5 will place the cursor on the fifth line in the file.

:$ - Positions the cursor on the last line of the file.

:set nu - Turn on line numbering.

:set nonu - Turn off line numbering.

:help [subcommand] - Get help. If you want more information on the   :w   command   type   :help   :w.

Mode	Key	Description
Command	Esc	Used to navigate, search, and copy/paste text.
Insert	i I a A	Also called text mode. Allows text to be inserted in the file.
Line	:	Also called command-line mode. Save the file, quit vi, replace text, and perform some navigation.

Here is a screenshot of vim. Tildes (~) represent lines beyond the end of the file.

```
                       bob@linuxsvr                    –  +  x
 File  Edit  View  Terminal  Tabs  Help
This is the first line.
This is the second.
Here is some more interesting text.
Knock knock.
Who's there?
More filler text.
The quick brown fox jumps over the lazy dog.
The dog was rather impressed.
Roses are red,
Violets are blue,
All my base are belong to you.
Finally, the 12th and last line.
~
~
~
"file.txt" 12L, 296C              1,1          All
```

Advanced Editing with vi

You can repeat commands in vi by preceding them with a number. For instance, if you would like to move the cursor up 5 lines type 5k. If you would like to insert a piece of text 80 times, type 80i and start entering the text. Once you hit Esc to return to command mode the text you typed will be repeated 80 times. If you would like to make a line of asterisks, you could type 80i*Esc. Can you start to see how vi is more powerful than an editor like nano?

Deleting Text

x - Delete a character.

dw - Delete a word. To delete five words, type d5w. The repeating concept in vi shows up in many places.

dd - Delete a line. To delete 3 lines, type 3dd.

D - Delete from the current position to the end of the line.

Changing Text

r - Replace the current character.

cw - Change the current word.

cc - Change the current line.

c$ - Change the text from the current position to the end of the line.

C - Same as c$.

~ - Reverses the case of a character.

Copying and Pasting

yy - Yank (copy) the current line.

y<position> - Yank the <position>. For example, to yank a word type yw. To yank three words type y3w.

p - Paste the most recent deleted or yanked text.

Undo / Redo

u - Undo.

Ctrl-r - Redo.

Searching

/<pattern> - Start a forward search for <pattern>.

?<pattern> - Start a reverse search for <pattern>.

Emacs

Emacs is another powerful editor. Some people really find themselves drawn to vi while others thoroughly enjoy using emacs. It's a bit of a rivalry in the Linux world, actually. Experiment with emacs and vi to see which one works for you. You can't make a bad choice as they are both great editors.

emacs [file] - Edit file.

When reading emacs documentation know that C-<char> means to hold down the Ctrl key while pressing <char>. For example, C-h means to hold down the Ctrl key while pressing the h key. If you see C-h t, that means to hold down Ctrl key while pressing the h key, release the Ctrl key and then type the letter t.

When you see M-<char>, that means hold down the "meta" key, which is the Alt key, while pressing <char>. You can also substitute the Esc key for the Alt key. So M-f translates to holding down the Alt key and pressing f or pressing and releasing Esc followed by typing the f key. You may need to use Esc for the meta key since Alt may be intercepted by your terminal program, for instance. If you want to simplify things, always use Esc for the meta key as it will work in all situations.

Here are some helpful emacs commands.

C-h - Help.

C-x C-c - Exit. While holding down Ctrl press x, continue to hold down Ctrl and press c.

C-x C-s - Save the file.

C-h t - Emacs has a nice built-in tutorial.

C-h k <key> - Describe key. Use this to get help on a specific key command or key combination.

Navigating

C-p - Previous line.

C-n - Next line.

C-b - Backward one character.

C-f - Forward one character.

M-f - Forward one word.

M-b - Backward one word.

C-a - Go to the beginning of the line.

C-e - Go to the end of the line.

M-< - Go to the beginning of the file.

M-> - Go to the end of the file.

Deleting Text

C-d - Delete a character.

M-d - Delete a word.

Copying and Pasting

C-k - Kill (cut) the rest of the current line of text. To kill the entire line, position the cursor at the beginning of the line.

C-y - Yank (or paste) from the previously killed text.

C-x u - Undo. Keep repeating for multi-level undo.

Searching

C-s - Start a forward search. Type the text you are looking for. Press C-s again to move to the next occurrence. Press Enter when you are done searching.

C-r - Start a reverse search.

Repeating

Like vi, emacs provides a way to repeat a command.

C-u N <command> - Repeat <command> N times.

For instance, to kill three lines of text type Ctrl-U 3 Ctrl-k.

You have only scratched the surface with the `vi` and `emacs` editors. There is so much more to learn if you are interested. Both editors have features that include macros, global replace, and more. Entire books have been written on each of the these editors.

Graphical Editors

So far you have learned about command line editors that are appropriate to use when you connect to a server via ssh. However, if you are running Linux as a desktop operating system you might be interesting in some graphical text editors and word processors. Here are some for your consideration.

- `emacs` - Emacs has a graphical mode, too.

- `gedit` - The default text editor for the Gnome desktop environment.

- `gvim` - The graphical version of `vim`.

- `kedit` - The default text editor for the KDE desktop environment.

If you are looking for a MicroSoft Word replacement, consider AbiWord or LibreOffice. LibreOffice not only includes a word processor, but it is a complete office suite with a spreadsheet program, a database, and presentation software.

If you are looking for a source code editor to aid in computer programming, look at Geany, jEdit, or Kate. Sublime Text is another option. It is a commercial product that runs on Windows, Mac, and Linux.

Specifying a Default Editor

Some commands rely on the $EDITOR environment variable to tell them which program to use for editing. Since cron's primary purpose is to schedule jobs, it delegates the task of editing files to another program. The crontab -e command invokes the editor specified by the $EDITOR environment variable. You can set $EDITOR in your personal initialization files to ensure your favorite editor is used, be it nano, emacs, vi, or something else.

```
$ echo $EDITOR
vi
```

Deep Dive

- Emacs How To - An emacs tutorial.
  http://help.ubuntu.com/community/EmacsHowto

- Emacs built-in tutorial - Start `emacs` and type `Ctrl-h t`.

- The Beginner's Guide to Nano
  http://www.howtogeek.com/howto/42980/

- Vi tutorial
  https://www.washington.edu/computing/unix/vi.html

- `vimtutor` - Run `vimtutor` from the command line start the vim tutorial.

- Welcome Back to Shell - The commands `more` and `less` are called pagers because they allow you to page through a file. You will learn more about them in the "Welcome Back to Shell" chapter.

COMPARING FILES

If you want to compare two files and display the differences you can use `diff`, `sdiff`, or `vimdiff`.

`diff file1 file2` - Compare two files.

`sdiff file1 file2` - Compare two files side by side.

`vimdiff file1 file2` - Highlight the differences between two files in the `vim` editor.

```
$ cat secret
site: facebook.com
user: bob
pass: Abee!
$ cat secret.bak
site: facebook.com
user: bob
pass: bee
$ diff secret secret.bak
3c3
```

```
< pass: Abee!
---
> pass: bee
$ sdiff secret secret.bak
site: facebook.com      site: facebook.com
user: bob               user: bob
pass: Abee!           | pass: bee
```

In the `diff` output, the text following the less-than sign (<) belongs to the first file. The text following the greater-than sign (>) belongs to the second file. The first line of the diff output provides some additional information. The first number represents line numbers from the first file and the second number represent lines from the second file. The middle character separating the line numbers will be a `c` meaning change, a `d` meaning deletion, or an `a` meaning an addition. In this example the third line of the first file is changed from "pass: Abee!" to the text on the third line in the second file which is "pass: bee."

In the sdiff output the pipe (|) character means that the text differs in the files on that line. You will also see the less-than sign (<) meaning that line only exists in the first file. The greater-than sign (>) means that line only exists in the second file.

Here is a screenshot of `vimdiff secret secret.bak` demonstrating how the changes are highlighted using color.

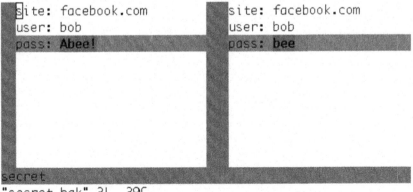

```
site: facebook.com       site: facebook.com
user: bob                user: bob
pass: Abee!              pass: bee



secret
"secret.bak" 3L, 39C
```

DETERMINING A FILE'S TYPE

There are clues as to what a file might contain. For instance, some files will have extensions. If a file ends in `.txt`, it is probably a text file. If a file has execute permissions, it might be a program. An easy way to determine the type of a file is to run the `file` command against it.

`file file` - Display the file type.

```
$ file /etc/passwd
/etc/passwd: ASCII text
$ file *
bin: directory
bob.tar: POSIX tar archive
test.data: data
test.txt: ASCII English text
email-reports.sh: Bourne-Again shell script, ASCII
text executable
```

SEARCHING IN FILES

Searching for Text in ASCII Files

If you are looking for text within a file, use the `grep` command.

`grep pattern file` - Search for pattern in file.

`grep -v pattern file` - Invert match. Return lines from file that do not match pattern.

```
$ cat secret
site: facebook.com
user: bob
pass: Abee!
$ grep user secret
user: bob
$ grep o secret
site: facebook.com
user: bob
$ grep -v o secret
pass: Abee!
```

Here are some more common options to use with grep.

`grep  -i` - Perform a search, ignoring case.

`grep  -c` - Count the number of occurrences in a file.

`grep  -n` - Precede output with line numbers from the file.

```
$ grep User secret
$ grep -i User secret
user: bob
$ grep -ci User secret
1
$ grep -ni User secret
2:user: bob
```

Searching For Text in Binary Files

If you run `grep` against a binary file, it will simply display whether or not that information was found in the file, but it will not display the surrounding text. To look at textual data within a binary file use the `strings` command.

`strings  file` - Display printable strings in binary files.

```
$ grep -i john BlueTrain.mp3
Binary file BlueTrain.mp3 matches
$ strings BlueTrain.mp3 | grep -i john
John Coltrane
John Coltrane
$
```

Pipes

You will notice that two commands have been chained together with a vertical bar, also known as the pipe symbol. The pipe (|) means take the standard output from the preceding command and pass it as the standard input to the following command. If the first command displays error messages those will not be passed to the second command. Those error messages are called "standard error" output. You will learn how to manipulate standard error output in the "Redirection" chapter.

Also notice that in the first occurrence of the `grep` command the format of `grep -i pattern file` was used. In the second, the format of `grep -i pattern` was used. In the first format the input for grep came from `file`. In the second format the input for grep came from the preceding command via the pipe.

If you run `strings BlueTrain.mp3` a lot of text will be displayed on the screen. Instead of letting that text pass you by, you can feed it to `grep -i john` using a pipe. The result, as you can see, is that 'John Coltrane' was found twice in the `strings BlueTrain.mp3` output.

Pipes aren't limited to just two commands. You can keep chaining commands together until you get the desired result you are looking for. Let's feed the output from `grep` to `head -1` to limit the output to just one line.

```
$ strings BlueTrain.mp3 | grep -i john | head -1
John Coltrane
$
```

Let's say you only want to display the second word of the above output. You can use the `cut` command to accomplish that goal.

`cut [file]` - Cut out selected portions of file. If file is omitted, use standard input.

`cut -d delimiter` - Use delimiter as the field separator.

`cut -f N` - Display the Nth field.

To extract 'Coltrane' from 'John Coltrane', use a space as the delimiter (`-d ' '`) and print the second field (`-f 2`). The space was quoted since spaces are typically ignored by the shell. Single quotes or double quotes work the same in this situation.

```
$ strings BlueTrain.mp3|grep -i john|head -1|cut -d ' ' -f2
Coltrane
$
```

You will find that there are many small commands that do just one thing well. Some examples are awk, cat, cut, fmt, join, less, more, nl, pr, sed, seq, sort, tr, and uniq. Let's take an example using some of those commands and chain them together with pipes.

The /etc/passwd file contains a list of accounts on the system and information about those accounts. In this example, the goal is to find all of the users named "bob" listed in the /etc/passwd file and print them in alphabetical order by username in a tabular format. Here is one way you could do that.

```
$ cd /etc
$ grep bob passwd
bob:x:1000:1000:Bob:/home/bob:/bin/bash
bobdjr:x:1001:1000:Robert
Downey:/home/bobdjr:/bin/bash
bobh:x:1002:1000:Bob Hope:/home/bobh:/bin/bash
bobs:x:1003:1000:Bob Saget:/home/bobs:/bin/bash
bobd:x:1004:1000:Bob Dylan:/home/bobd:/bin/bash
bobb:x:1005:1000:Bob Barker:/home/bobb:/bin/bash
$ grep bob passwd | cut -f1,5 -d:
bob:Bob
bobdjr:Robert Downey
bobh:Bob Hope
bobs:Bob Saget
bobd:Bob Dylan
bobb:Bob Barker
$ grep bob passwd | cut -f1,5 -d: | sort
bob:Bob
bobb:Bob Barker
bobd:Bob Dylan
bobdjr:Robert Downey
bobh:Bob Hope
```

```
bobs:Bob Saget
$ grep bob passwd | cut -f1,5 -d: | sort | sed 's/:/ /'
bob Bob
bobb Bob Barker
bobd Bob Dylan
bobdjr Robert Downey
bobh Bob Hope
bobs Bob Saget
$ grep bob passwd | cut -f1,5 -d: | sort | sed 's/:/ /' |column -t
bob       Bob
bobb      Bob       Barker
bobd      Bob       Dylan
bobdjr    Robert    Downey
bobh      Bob       Hope
bobs      Bob       Saget
```

The above example shows the step-by-step thought process of how to go from one set of output and pipe it as the input to the next command. If you need to perform this action often you could save the final command for later use. As you can see, this simple concept of piping makes Linux extremely powerful.

Pipe Output to a Pager

Another common use of pipes is to control how output is displayed to your screen. If a command produces a significant amount of output it can scroll off your screen before you have the chance to examine it. To control the output use a pager utility such as more or less. You've already used those commands directly on files, but keep in mind they can take redirected input too.

```
$ grep bob /etc/passwd | less
bob:x:1000:1000:Bob:/home/bob:/bin/bash
bobdjr:x:1001:1000:Robert
Downey:/home/bobdjr:/bin/bash
bobh:x:1002:1000:Bob Hope:/home/bobh:/bin/bash
bobb:x:1005:1000:Bob Barker:/home/bobb:/bin/bash
```

```
...
$ ls -l /usr/bin | less
total 62896
-rwxr-xr-x 1 root root  35264 Nov 19  2012 [
-rwxr-xr-x 1 root root     96 Sep 26 20:28 2to3-2.7
-rwxr-xr-x 1 root root     96 Sep 25 18:23 2to3-3.2
-rwxr-xr-x 1 root root  16224 Mar 18  2013 a2p
-rwxr-xr-x 1 root root  55336 Jul 12  2013 ab
....
$ ps -ef | more
UID    PID  PPID  C STIME TTY       TIME CMD
root     1     0  0 Jan08 ?     00:00:00 /sbin/init
root     2     0  0 Jan08 ?     00:00:00 [kthreadd]
root     3     2  0 Jan08 ?     00:00:01 [ksoftirqd/0]
root     6     2  0 Jan08 ?     00:00:00 [migration/0]
root     7     2  0 Jan08 ?     00:00:04 [watchdog/0]
...
$
```

DAY 4

DELETING, COPYING, MOVING, AND RENAMING FILES

Removing Files

Eventually you will get tired of all the old files you created just laying around, cluttering up your home directory, and taking up precious space. To delete them, use the rm command.

rm file - Remove file.

rm -r directory - Remove the directory and its contents recursively. If you want to remove a directory with rm, you have to supply the -r argument.

rm -f file - Force removal and never prompt for confirmation.

Search patterns can be used to delete multiple files at once. It's a good idea to double check what you are going to remove with ls before you execute rm.

```
$ ls s*
sales-lecture.mp3 sales.data secret secret.bak
$ rm s*
$ ls -d .*
.  ..  .profile .bash_history
$ rm .*
rm: cannot remove '.': Is a directory
rm: cannot remove '..': Is a directory
$ ls -d .*
.  ..
```

Note that rm .* will not remove . (this directory) and .. (the parent directory).

Copying Files

To copy files, use the cp command. If you want to create a copy of a file you can run cp source_file destination_file. You can also copy a file, or a series of files, to a directory by using cp file(s) dir.

cp source_file destination_file - Copy source_file to destination_file.

cp source_file1 [source_fileN ...] destination_directory - Copy source_files to destination_directory.

cp -i source_file destination_file - Run cp in interactive mode. If the destination_file exists, cp will prompt you before it overwrites the file.

cp -r source_directory destination - Copy source_directory recursively to destination. If destination exists, copy source_directory into destination, otherwise create destination with the contents of directory.

```
$ cp file1 file2
$ mkdir dir
$ cp file1 file2 dir/
$ ls dir
file1 file2
$ rm dir/*
$ cp file1 file2 dir
$ cp -i file1 file2
overwrite file2? (y/n [n]) n
not overwritten
$ cp -r dir dir2
$ ls dir2
file1 file2
$ cp dir dir3
cp: dir is a directory (not copied).
$ mkdir dir3
$ cp -r dir dir2 dir3
$ ls dir3
dir  dir2
$ tree dir3
dir3
├── dir
│   ├── file1
│   └── file2
└── dir2
    ├── file1
    └── file2
```

Moving and Renaming Files

The way to rename files or directories in Linux is to use the mv command. The mv command moves files from one location to another. This can be used to relocate files or directories and it can be used to rename them also.

mv source destination - Move files or directories. If destination is a directory, source will be moved into destination. Otherwise source will be renamed to destination.

118

mv -i source destination - Run mv in interactive mode. If the destination exists, mv will prompt you before it overwrites the file.

Look at the following examples. They should make it clear how the mv command behaves in various situations.

```
$ ls -F
dir/    dir2/  dir3/  file1  file2
$ mv dir firstdir
$ ls -F
dir2/       dir3/        file1        file2        firstdir/
$ mv file1 file1.renamed
$ ls -F
dir2/            dir3/            file1.renamed  file2
firstdir/
$ mv file1.renamed firstdir/
$ ls -F
dir2/       dir3/       file2       firstdir/
$ ls -F firstdir/
file1           file1.renamed  file2
$ cat firstdir/file1
This text started out in file1.
$ cat firstdir/file2
This text started out in file2.
$ mv firstdir/file1 firstdir/file2
$ cat firstdir/file2
This text started out in file1.
$ ls -F firstdir/
file1.renamed  file2
$ mv -i firstdir/file1.renamed firstdir/file2
overwrite firstdir/file2? (y/n [n]) n
not overwritten
$
```

In the above example, a directory was renamed with mv dir firstdir. Next, a file was renamed with mv file file1.renamed. Next file1.renamed was relocated to the firstdir directory with the mv file1.renamed firstdir/ command. A file was overwritten with the mv firstdir/file1 `firstdir/file2` command. If you want to be prompted before a file is overwritten use the `-i` option.

SORTING DATA

You have already seen the sort command in use. In the simplest form it sorts lines of text alphabetically.

sort file - Sort text in file.

sort -k F file - Sort by key. The F following -k is the field number.

sort -r file - Sort in reverse order.

sort -u file - Sort text in file, removing duplicate lines.

```
$ cat more-secrets
tags: credentials
site: facebook.com
user: bob
pass: Abee!
tags: credentials
$ sort more-secrets
pass: Abee!
site: facebook.com
tags: credentials
tags: credentials
user: bob
$ sort -u more-secrets
pass: Abee!
site: facebook.com
tags: credentials
user: bob
$ sort -ru more-secrets
user: bob
tags: credentials
site: facebook.com
pass: Abee!
$ sort -u -k2 more-secrets
pass: Abee!
user: bob
tags: credentials
site: facebook.com
```

CREATING A COLLECTION OF FILES

If you want to bundle a group of files and/or directories together in an archive, you can use the `tar` command. You may want to create a copy or backup of a group of files. You may have several files you want to transfer at once or as a set. In these situations, `tar` can help.

`tar [-] c|x|t f tarfile [pattern]` - Create, extract or list contents of a tar archive using pattern, if supplied.

You will notice that tar does not require a hyphen (-) to precede its arguments. Traditionally the hyphen is excluded, but tar still works with it. If you see `tar cf file.tar` it is the same as `tar -cf file.tar`. Here is a look at some of the most commonly used tar options.

`c` - Create a tar archive.

`x` - Extract files from the archive.

`t` - Display the table of contents (list).

`v` - Causes `tar` to be verbose.

f file - The tar archive file to perform operations against.

In the following example tar is used to create (tar cf tps.tar) an archive, list the contents of the archive (tar tf tps.tar) and extract the contents (tar xf tps.tar).

```
$ tar cf tps.tar tpsreports/
$ tar tf tps.tar
tpsreports/
tpsreports/sales-report.txt
tpsreports/coversheet.doc
$ cd /tmp
$ tar xf /home/bob/tps.tar
$ ls tpsreports/
coversheet.doc sales-report.txt
$
```

If you would like to see the files that are getting placed into the archive or extracted from the archive, use -v to enable verbose mode.

```
$ tar cvf misc.tar sec* tpsreports
secret
secret.bak
tpsreports/
tpsreports/sales-report.txt
tpsreports/coversheet.doc
$ tar xvf /home/bob/misc.tar
secret
secret.bak
tpsreports/
tpsreports/sales-report.txt
tpsreports/coversheet.doc
```

COMPRESSING FILES TO SAVE SPACE

`gzip file` - Compress file. The resulting compressed file is named file.gz.

`gunzip file` - Uncompress files.

`gzcat` or `zcat` - Concatenates and prints compressed files.

You can use the command `du` to display how much space is used by a file.

`du` - Estimates file usage.

`du -k` - Display sizes in Kilobytes.

`du -h` - Display sizes in human readable format. For example, 1.2M, 3.7G, etc.

Here are a couple of quick examples that demonstrate how to compress and uncompress files.

```
$ du -k data
15360 data
$ gzip data
$ du -k data.gz
26 data.gz
$ ls data*
data.gz
$ gunzip data.gz
$ ls data*
data
$ du -k misc.tar
10 misc.tar
$ gzip misc.tar
$ du -k misc.tar*
misc.tar.gz
$
```

COMPRESSING ARCHIVES

In modern versions of the `tar` command `gzip` compression is built-in. If you want to create, extract, or list the contents of a compressed archive use the `-z` argument. As a matter of convention compressed tar files will end in either `.tar.gz` or `.tgz`. Here is how this looks.

```
$ tar zcf tps.tgz tpsreports
$ ls *.tgz
tps.tgz
$ tar ztf tps.tgz
tpsreports/
tpsreports/sales-report.txt
tpsreports/coversheet.doc
$
```

If you run across an older version of `tar` without gzip compression built-in, you can use pipes to create compressed archives. When a hyphen (–) is used in place of a file name that means to use standard output. Running the command `tar cf - pattern` will create an archive of "pattern" and send the output to standard output which is normally your screen. If you follow the command with a pipe that standard output will be used as the input for the next command following the pipe. To force gunzip to send its output to standard out, use the −c argument. With this in mind, here is how you can create, list, and extract a compressed archive using tar, gzip, and pipes.

```
$ tar cf - tpsreports | gzip > tps.tgz
$ ls *.tgz
tps.tgz
$ gunzip -c tps.tgz | tar tf -
tpsreports/
tpsreports/sales-report.txt
tpsreports/coversheet.doc
$ cd /tmp
$ gunzip -c /home/bob/tps.tgz | tar xf -
$ ls tpsreports/
coversheet.doc sales-report.txt
$
```

REDIRECTION

You have already learned how to redirect output from one command and send it as input to another one by using pipes. In the previous example you saw another way to redirect output using the greater-than (>) sign. Let's take a closer look at I/O (input/output) redirection.

There are three default types of input and output. They are standard input, standard output, and standard error. By default, standard input comes from the keyboard and standard output and standard error are displayed to the screen. Each one of these I/O types is given a file descriptor. File descriptors are just numbers that represent open files. For humans it is easier for us to reference files by name, but it is easier for computers to reference them by number.

You may be thinking, "my keyboard isn't a file, nor is my screen." On one level that is true, but on another level it is not. Linux represents practically everything as a file. This abstraction allows you to do powerful things like take the standard output of one command that would normally be displayed to your screen and use it as input to another command. It's easier to run `cat file.txt | sort` than it is to type the entire contents of `file.txt` as the input to the `sort` command.

To demonstrate this concept, run `sort`, type in some text, and press `Ctrl-d` on a blank line. Here is how that looks.

```
$ sort
dddd
a
ccc
bb
<<<< Type Ctrl-d here >>>>
a
bb
ccc
dddd
$ cat file.txt
dddd
a
ccc
bb
$ cat file.txt | sort
a
bb
ccc
dddd
$
```

I/O Name	Abbreviation	File Descriptor Number
standard input	stdin	0
standard output	stdout	1
standard error	stderr	2

Use the greater-than sign (>) to redirect output and the less-than sign (<) to redirect input. The explicit way of using redirection is to provide a file descriptor number, however if it is omitted then file descriptor 0 is assumed for input redirection and 1 for output redirection.

> - Redirects standard output to a file, overwriting (truncating) any existing contents of the file. If no file exists, it creates one.

>> - Redirects standard output to a file and appends to any existing contents. If no file exists, it creates one.

< - Redirects input from a file to the command preceding the less-than sign.

```
$ ls -lF /opt/apache
drwxr-xr-x 2 root root 4096 Sep 14 12:21 2.3
drwxr-xr-x 2 root root 4096 Nov 27 15:43 2.4
lrwxrwxrwx 1 root root    5 Nov 27 15:43 current -> 2.4
-rw-r--r-- 1 root root 1048 Sep 14 12:58 README
$ ls -lF /opt/apache > files.txt
$ cat files.txt
drwxr-xr-x 2 root root 4096 Sep 14 12:21 2.3
drwxr-xr-x 2 root root 4096 Nov 27 15:43 2.4
lrwxrwxrwx 1 root root    5 Nov 27 15:43 current -> 2.4
-rw-r--r-- 1 root root 1048 Sep 14 12:58 README
$ ls -lF /opt/apache >> files.txt
$ cat files.txt
drwxr-xr-x 2 root root 4096 Sep 14 12:21 2.3
drwxr-xr-x 2 root root 4096 Nov 27 15:43 2.4
lrwxrwxrwx 1 root root    5 Nov 27 15:43 current -> 2.4
-rw-r--r-- 1 root root 1048 Sep 14 12:58 README
drwxr-xr-x 2 root root 4096 Sep 14 12:21 2.3
drwxr-xr-x 2 root root 4096 Nov 27 15:43 2.4
lrwxrwxrwx 1 root root    5 Nov 27 15:43 current -> 2.4
-rw-r--r-- 1 root root 1048 Sep 14 12:58 README
$ sort < files.txt
-rw-r--r-- 1 root root 1048 Sep 14 12:58 README
-rw-r--r-- 1 root root 1048 Sep 14 12:58 README
drwxr-xr-x 2 root root 4096 Nov 27 15:43 2.3
drwxr-xr-x 2 root root 4096 Nov 27 15:43 2.3
drwxr-xr-x 2 root root 4096 Sep 14 12:21 2.4
drwxr-xr-x 2 root root 4096 Sep 14 12:21 2.4
```

```
lrwxrwxrwx 1 root root     5 Nov 27 15:43 current -> 2.4
lrwxrwxrwx 1 root root     5 Nov 27 15:43 current -> 2.4
```

In the above examples `ls -lF /opt/apache > files.txt` is the same as `ls -lF /opt/apache 1> files.txt`. Also, `sort < files.txt` is the same as `sort 0< files.txt`. Do not use a space between the file descriptor number and the redirection operator. The file descriptor must immediately precede the redirection operator, otherwise it will be interpreted as another item on the command line.

```
$ ls -lF /opt/apache 1 > files.txt
ls: 1: No such file or directory
$ ls -lF /opt/apache 1> files.txt
$ sort 0 < files.txt
sort: open failed: 0: No such file or directory
$ sort 0< files.txt
-rw-r--r-- 1 root root 1048 Sep 14 12:58 README
-rw-r--r-- 1 root root 1048 Sep 14 12:58 README
drwxr-xr-x 2 root root 4096 Nov 27 15:43 2.3
drwxr-xr-x 2 root root 4096 Nov 27 15:43 2.3
drwxr-xr-x 2 root root 4096 Sep 14 12:21 2.4
drwxr-xr-x 2 root root 4096 Sep 14 12:21 2.4
lrwxrwxrwx 1 root root     5 Nov 27 15:43 current -> 2.4
lrwxrwxrwx 1 root root     5 Nov 27 15:43 current -> 2.4
$
```

Input and output redirection can be combined. This example shows `files.txt` being redirected as input for the `sort` command. The output of the `sort` command is then redirected to the `sorted_files.txt` file.

```
$ sort < files.txt > sorted_files.txt
$ cat sorted_files.txt
-rw-r--r-- 1 root root 1048 Sep 14 12:58 README
-rw-r--r-- 1 root root 1048 Sep 14 12:58 README
drwxr-xr-x 2 root root 4096 Nov 27 15:43 2.3
drwxr-xr-x 2 root root 4096 Nov 27 15:43 2.3
drwxr-xr-x 2 root root 4096 Sep 14 12:21 2.4
drwxr-xr-x 2 root root 4096 Sep 14 12:21 2.4
lrwxrwxrwx 1 root root     5 Nov 27 15:43 current -> 2.4
```

```
lrwxrwxrwx 1 root root     5 Nov 27 15:43 current -> 2.4
```

Standard Error

When a program encounters an error it reports its findings to standard error. File descriptor 1 is for standard output, 2 is for standard error. Remember that file descriptor 1 is the default file descriptor for output redirection. This can mean that not all of the output generated by a program is captured by default. Here is an example.

```
$ ls here not-here
ls: not-here: No such file or directory
here
$ ls here not-here > out
ls: not-here: No such file or directory
$ cat out
here
$ ls here not-here 2> out.err
here

$ cat out.err
ls: not-here: No such file or directory
$ ls here not-here 1> out 2> out.err
$ cat out
here
$ cat out.err
ls: not-here: No such file or directory
$
```

You will notice that when using > the error message was displayed to the screen and not redirected to the out file. To redirect the error messages you had to explicitly specify file descriptor 2 with 2>. You can send standard output to one file while sending standard error to another file. You can use this to your advantage by having one file that contains known good output and another file that you can examine for errors.

If you want to capture both standard output and standard error, use

2>&1. Normally with redirection a file follows the redirection operator. If you want to use a file descriptor instead of a file name, use the ampersand (&) symbol. So instead of redirecting standard error to a file (2>out.err), redirect it to standard output (2>&1). If you omit &, 1 will be treated as a file named 1.

& - Used with redirection to signal that a file descriptor is being used instead of a file name.

2>&1 - Combine standard error and standard output.

2> file - Redirect standard error to a file.

```
$ ls here not-here > out.both 2>&1
$ cat out.both
ls: not-here: No such file or directory
here
$
```

The command, ls here not-here > out.both 2>&1 means "send the standard output of ls here not-here to file the named out.both and append standard error to standard output." Since standard error is redirected to standard output and standard output is redirected to out.both, all output will be written to out.both.

Null Device

>/dev/null - Redirect output to nowhere.

If you want to ignore output, you can send it to the null device, /dev/null. The null device is a special file that throws away whatever is fed to it. You may hear people refer to it as the bit bucket. If you do not want to see errors on your screen and you do not want to save them to a file, you can redirect them to /dev/null.

```
$ ls here not-here 2> /dev/null
here
```

```
$ ls here not-here > /dev/null 2>&1
$
```

Deep Dive

- File Descriptors http://en.wikipedia.org/wiki/File_descriptor

- Here Documents
  http://en.wikipedia.org/wiki/Here-document

- Null Device
  http://en.wikipedia.org/wiki//dev/null

- Redirection
  http://en.wikipedia.org/wiki/Redirection_(computing)

TRANSFERRING AND COPYING FILES

You already know how to copy files from one location to another on the same system using the `cp` command. But what if you want to copy files from your local workstation to a Linux server or between Linux servers? For that you can use SCP or SFTP.

SCP is secure copy and SFTP is SSH file transfer protocol. Sometimes SFTP is referred to as secure file transfer protocol. SCP and SFTP are both extensions of the secure shell (SSH) protocol. This means that if you have SSH key authentication configured for SSH, it will also work with SCP and SFTP.

In order to use SCP or SFTP you need a client. Mac and Linux come with `scp` and `sftp` command line utilities. If you are running Windows, you can use the PuTTY Secure Copy Client (`pscp.exe`) and the PuTTY Secure File Transfer client (`psftp.exe`) programs. Command line utilities aren't your only option. There are graphical clients for each platform as well. Some run on Windows, Linux, and Mac like FileZilla, while others only run on one platform like WinSCP for Windows.

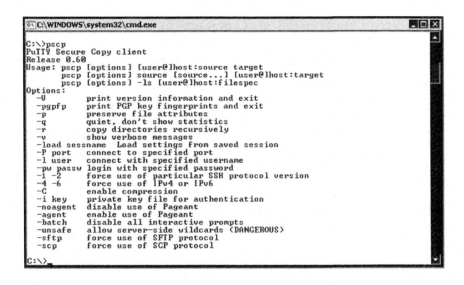

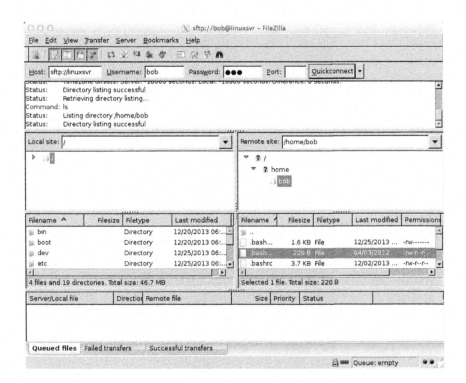

`scp source destination` - **Copy source to destination.**

`sftp [username@]host` - **Connect to host as username to begin a secure file transfer session.**

If you are looking for a more interactive experience where you can examine the local and remote file systems, use SFTP. With SCP you need to know what files you want to transfer before using the command. Here is a sample SFTP session.

```
bobby@laptop:/tmp $ sftp bob@linuxsvr
bob@linuxsvr's password:
Connected to linuxsvr.
sftp> pwd
Remote working directory: /home/bob
sftp> ls -la
drwxr-xr-x    4 bob   bob   4096 Dec 25 19:00 .
drwxr-xr-x    4 root  root  4096 Dec  2 22:01 ..
-rw-r--r--    1 bob   bob   3655 Dec  2 22:02 .bashrc
-rw-r--r--    1 bob   bob    675 Apr  3 2012 .profile
drwx------    2 bob   bob   4096 Dec 25 19:00 .ssh
sftp> lpwd
Local working directory: /tmp
sftp> lls
file1.txt
sftp> put file1.txt
Uploading file1.txt to /home/bob/file1.txt
file1.txt
100%    18       0.0KB/s    00:00
sftp> ls
file1.txt
sftp> ls -la
drwxr-xr-x    4 bob   bob   4096 Dec 25 19:02 .
drwxr-xr-x    4 root  root  4096 Dec  2 22:01 ..
-rw-r--r--    1 bob   bob   3655 Dec  2 22:02 .bashrc
-rw-r--r--    1 bob   bob    675 Apr  3 2012 .profile
drwx------    2 bob   bob   4096 Dec 25 19:00 .ssh
-rw-rw-r--    1 bob   bob     18 Dec 25 19:02 file1.txt
sftp> quit
```

Using `scp`, you can copy from your local system to a remote system, from a remote system to your local system, or from one remote system to another remote system. Here is how that looks.

```
$ scp test.txt linuxsvr1:~/
test.txt       100%    35KB   35.3KB/s     00:00
$ scp linuxsvr1:~/test.txt .
test.txt       100%    35KB   35.3KB/s     00:00
$ scp linuxsvr1:~/test.txt linuxsvr2:/tmp/test-copy.txt
$
```

SCP and SFTP aren't the only ways to transfer files to remote systems. Sometimes FTP (file transfer protocol) is enabled. In such cases you can use the built-in `ftp` command on Linux and Mac and a graphical client like WinSCP for windows. Just be aware that FTP is not using a secure transfer protocol like SCP and SFTP. This means that your login credentials are sent in plain text over the network. Also, the files that you upload and download are not encrypted either. If given the choice between SCP/SFTP or FTP, use SCP/SFTP.

```
bobby@laptop:~$ ftp linuxsvr
Connected to linuxsvr.
220 ubuntu FTP server (Version 6.4) ready.
Name (linuxsvr:bobby): bob
331 Password required for bob.
Password:
230 User bob logged in.
Remote system type is UNIX.
Using binary mode to transfer files.
ftp> pwd
257 "/home/bob" is current directory.
ftp> quit
221 Goodbye.
```

If FTP is not enabled, you will see a "Connection refused" error message.

```
bobby@laptop:~$ ftp linuxsvr
ftp: connect: Connection refused
ftp> quit
bobby@laptop:~$
```

Deep dive

- Connecting via SSH with Keys - SSH key information covered earlier in this book.

- Cyberduck - FTP and SFTP client for Mac and Windows. http://cyberduck.io/

- FileZilla - FTP and SFTP client for Mac, Linux, and Windows. https://filezilla-project.org/

- FireFTP - FTP and SFTP client Firefox that is Mac, Linux, and Windows compatible. http://fireftp.net/

- PuTTY http://www.LinuxTrainingAcademy.com/putty/

    - PSCP.EXE - SCP client for Windows

    - PSFTP.EXE - SFTP client for Windows

- Transmit - FTP and SFTP client for Mac. http://www.panic.com/transmit/

- WinSCP - FTP and SFTP client for Windows. http://winscp.net/

Customizing the Prompt

As you have seen in the "Welcome To Shell" chapter, default prompts can vary from system to system. No matter what shell you are using, you can customize your prompt by setting an environment variable. For shells like `bash`, `ksh`, and `sh` the environment variable `PS1` is used to set the primary prompt string. The shells `csh`, `tcsh`, and `zsh` use the `prompt` environment variable. The format string you place in the environment variable determines the look and feel of your prompt. Each shell uses different format strings so consult the documentation for the shell that you are using.

Let's look at customizing the bash prompt since bash is the most popular default shell for user accounts on Linux systems. These are some of the commonly used formatting string options for bash. For a complete list refer to the man page.

\d - the date in "Weekday Month Date" format (e.g., "Tue May 26")

\h - the hostname up to the first '.'

\H - the hostname

\n - newline

\t - the current time in 24-hour HH:MM:SS format

\T - the current time in 12-hour HH:MM:SS format

\@ - the current time in 12-hour am/pm format

\A - the current time in 24-hour HH:MM format

\u - the username of the current user

\w - the current working directory, with $HOME abbreviated with a tilde

\W - the basename of the current working directory, with $HOME abbreviated with a tilde

\$ - if the effective UID is 0, a #, otherwise a $

Here are some examples of changing the bash shell prompt by manipulating the PS1 environment variable.

```
[bob@linuxsvr ~]$ echo $PS1
[\u@\h \w]\$
[bob@linuxsvr ~]$ PS1="\u@\h \$ "
bob@linuxsvr $ PS1="<\t \u@\h \w>\$ "
<16:42:58 bob@linuxsvr ~>$ cd /tmp
<16:43:02 bob@linuxsvr /tmp>$ PS1="\d \t \h \W>\$ "
Mon Nov 18 16:45:51 linuxsvr tmp>$ PS1="\t\n[\h \w]\$ "
16:46:47
[linuxsvr /tmp]$
```

To make your customized shell prompt persist betweens logins, add the PS1 value to your personal initialization files. Personal initialization files are commonly referred to as "dot files" since they begin with a dot or period.

```
$ echo 'export PS1="[\u@\h \w]\$ "' >>
~/.bash_profile
```

Creating Aliases

If you find yourself typing the same command over and over again, you can create a shortcut for it called an alias. An alias can be thought of as a text expander. Creating aliases for commands that are really long is also a common practice. For example, if you type ls -l frequently, you may want to abbreviate it to ll. As a matter of fact, this alias often comes predefined on many Linux distributions.

alias [name[=value]] - List or create aliases. If no arguments are provided the current list of aliases is displayed. Use name=value to create a new alias.

```
$ ls -l
total 4
-rw-r--r-- 1 bob bob 221 Nov 13 11:30 file.txt
$ alias ll='ls -l'
$ ll
total 4
-rw-r--r-- 1 bob bob 221 Nov 13 11:30 file.txt
$ alias
alias egrep='egrep --color=auto'
alias fgrep='fgrep --color=auto'
alias grep='grep --color=auto'
alias l='ls -CF'
alias la='ls -A'
alias ll='ls -l'
alias ls='ls --color=auto'
$
```

You can even use aliases to fix common typing errors. If you find yourself typing grpe when you intend to type grep, create an alias.

```
$ alias grpe='grep'
```

Aliases can be created to make your work environment similar to that of another platform. For instance, in Windows `cls` clears the screen, but in Linux the equivalent command is `clear`. If you are coming from an HP-UX background you are most likely familiar with the command `bdf` which displays disk usage. On Linux a very similar command is `df`. You could create these shortcuts to help you feel more at home.

```
$ alias cls='clear'
$ alias bdf='df'
```

Note that if you were to log out and log back in, your aliases would be lost. To make them persist between sessions add them to one of your personal initialization files (dot files) like `.bash_profile`.

The downside to creating several aliases is that when you are on a system that does not have your aliases you might feel lost. If you want to be able to work effectively on any system that you have access to, keep your alias usage to a minimum. Another way to handle this situation is to copy your configuration files to each system that you work on.

Interactive vs Non-interactive Sessions

The shell behaves in slightly different ways when you log on interactively versus when you just connect to run a single command. Here is an example to better illustrate the difference between interactive and non-interactive shells.

Interactive:

```
mac:~ bob$ ssh linuxsvr
Last login: Thu Nov  7 01:26:37 UTC 2013
Welcome to Ubuntu 12.04.3 LTS

 * Documentation:  https://help.ubuntu.com/

   System info as of Nov 14 01:26:52 UTC 2013

   System load:  0.42
```

```
Usage of /:    3.1% of 40GB
Memory usage: 32%
Swap usage:    0%
Processes:             89
Users logged in:       0
IP address for eth0: 10.0.0.7

bob@linuxsvr:~$ uptime
 11:49:16 up 97 days,  2:59,  5 users,  load average:
0.15, 0.25, 0.31

bob@linuxsvr:~$ ll
-rw-r--r-- 1 bob bob 221 Nov 13 11:30 file.txt
bob@linuxsvr:~$ exit
logout
Connection to 10.0.0.7 closed.
mac:~ bob$
```

Non interactive:

```
mac:~ bob$ ssh linuxsvr uptime
 11:49:16 up 97 days,  2:59,  5 users,  load average:
0.15, 0.25, 0.31
mac:~ bob$ ssh linuxsvr ll
bash: ll: command not found
mac:~ bob$
```

The contents of .profile or .bash_profile are only executed for interactive sessions. If you are not aware of this subtle difference it may leave you scratching your head as to why something works perfectly when you log in and type a command versus when you just ssh in to run that same command. For example, if you define an alias for ll in ~/.bash_profile it will work during an interactive session but it will not be available during a non-interactive session.

You can save yourself some hassle by making your interactive and non-interactive sessions behave the same. To do this, configure .bash_profile to reference .bashrc and put all of your configuration in .bashrc. You can read in the contents of another file by using the `source` command or dot operator.

`source filename` - Read and execute commands from filename and return. Any variables created or modified in filename will remain available after the script completes.

`. filename` - Same as `source filename`.

```
$ cat .bash_profile
# Put our settings in .bashrc so we have the same
environment for login and non-login shells.
if [ -f ~/.bashrc ]; then
    source ~/.bashrc
fi
$ cat .bashrc
# use a vi-style line editing interface
set -o vi

# Set the prompt.
PS1="[\u@\h \w]\$ "
export PS1

# Set the PATH.
PATH=$PATH:~/bin
export PATH

# Aliases
alias grpe='grep'
alias ll='ls -l'
alias utc='TZ=UTC date'
alias vi='vim'
```

Now the aliases you have defined are available during interactive and non-interactive sessions. Here is how the sessions behave after this change.

Interactive:

```
mac:~ bob$ ssh linuxsvr
Last login: Thu Nov  7 01:26:37 UTC 2013
Welcome to Ubuntu 12.04.3 LTS

 * Documentation:  https://help.ubuntu.com/

  System info as of Nov 14 01:26:52 UTC 2013

  System load:  0.42
  Usage of /:   3.1% of 40GB
  Memory usage: 32%
  Swap usage:   0%
  Processes:         89
  Users logged in:   0
  IP address for eth0: 10.0.0.7

bob@linuxsvr:~$ ll
-rw-r--r-- 1 bob bob 221 Nov 13 11:30 file.txt
bob@linuxsvr:~$ exit
logout
Connection to 10.0.0.7 closed.
mac:~ bob$
```

Non interactive:

```
mac:~ bob$ ssh linuxsvr ll
-rw-r--r-- 1 bob bob 221 Nov 13 11:30 file.txt
mac:~ bob$
```

Comments

In the above examples you might have noticed the octothorpe (#) followed by some very human like text in the ~/.bash_profile and ~/.bashrc files. Any text that follows an octothorpe is ignored by the shell. This is a very common pattern that not only works for shells, but also for several computer programming languages. This construct allows comments and annotations to be used without effecting the execution of a program or script.

- Octothorpe. Also known as a hash, square, pound sign, or number sign. This symbol precedes comments.

```
$ # This does nothing.
$ This does something.
This: command not found
$ alias # Show my aliases.
alias egrep='egrep --color=auto'
alias fgrep='fgrep --color=auto'
alias grep='grep --color=auto'
alias l='ls -CF'
alias la='ls -A'
alias ll='ls -l'
alias ls='ls --color=auto'
$
```

Shell History

The shell keeps a record of the commands you have previously executed. Bash keeps its history in memory for the current session and in the ~/.bash_history file so that it can be recalled during future sessions. Other shells may use ~/.history, ~/.zsh_history, or other similarly named files. Having access to your shell history is extremely useful because it allows you to quickly repeat commands. This can save you time, save keystrokes, prevent you from making mistakes by running a previously known good command, and generally speed up your work flow.

history - Display a list of commands in the shell history.

!N - Repeat command line number N.

!! - Repeat the previous command line.

!string - Repeat the most recent command starting with "string."

```
$ history
1 ls
2 diff secret secret.bak
3 history
$ !1
ls
PerformanceReviews tpsreports
$ echo $SHELL
/bin/bash
$ !!
echo $SHELL
/bin/bash
$ !d
diff secret secret.bak
3c3
< pass: Abee!
---
> pass: bee
$
```

With the exclamation mark history expansion syntax you can rerun a command by number. In the above example the first command in the history was executed with !1. If you want to execute the second command you would execute !2. Another convenient shortcut is !-N which means execute the Nth previous command. If you want to execute the second to last command type !-2. Since !! repeats the most recent command, it is the same as !-1.

```
$ history
1 ls
2 diff secret secret.bak
3 history
$ !-2
diff secret secret.bak
3c3
< pass: Abee!
---
> pass: bee
$
```

By default bash retains 500 commands in your shell history. This is controlled by the HISTSIZE environment variable. If you want to increase this number add export HISTSIZE=1000 or something similar to your personal initialization files.

Ctrl-r - Reverse search. Search for commands in your shell history.

You can search for commands in your history. For example, if you have the command find /var/tmp -type f in your shell history you could find it by typing Ctrl-r fi Enter. Ctrl-r initiates the reverse search and displays the search prompt, fi is the search string, and Enter executes the command that was found. You do not have to search for the start of the string. You could have very well searched for "var", "tmp", or "type."

```
$ find /var/tmp -type f
/var/tmp/file.txt
(reverse-i-search)`fi': find /var/tmp -type f
/var/tmp/file.txt
```

Tab Completion

Another way to increase your efficiency at the shell is by using tab completion. After you start typing a command you can hit the Tab key to invoke tab completion. Tab attempts to automatically complete partially typed commands. If there are multiple commands that begin with the string that precedes Tab, those commands will be displayed. You can continue to type and press Tab again. When there is only one possibility remaining, pressing the Tab key will complete the command.

Tab - Autocompletes commands and filenames.

```
$ # Typing who[Tab][Tab] results in:
$ who
who      whoami
$ # Typing whoa[Tab][Enter] results in:
$ whoami
bob
$
```

Tab completion not only works on commands, but it also works on files and directories. If you have files that start with a common prefix, Tab will expand the common component. For example, if you have two files named file1.txt and file2.txt, typing cat f Tab will expand the command line to cat file. You can then continue typing or press Tab twice to list the possible expansions. Typing cat f Tab 2 Tab will expand to cat file2.txt. After you experiment with tab completion it will soon become second nature.

```
$ # Typing cat f[Tab] results in:
$ cat file
$ # Typing: cat f[Tab][Tab][Tab] results in:
$ cat file
file1.txt  file2.txt
$ # Typing cat f[Tab] 2[Tab][Enter] results in:
$ cat file2.txt
This is file2!!!
$
```

Shell Command Line Editing

From time to time you will want to change something on your current command line. Maybe you noticed a spelling mistake at the front of the line or need to add an additional option to the current command. You may also find yourself wanting to recall a command from your shell history and modify it slightly to fit the current situation. Command line editing makes these types of activities possible.

Shells such as bash, ksh, tcsh, and zsh provide two command line editing modes. They are emacs, which is typically the default mode, and vi. Depending on the shell you can change editing modes by using the `set` or `bindkey` command. If you want to ensure your preferred mode is set upon login, add one of the two commands to your personal initialization files.

Shell	Emacs Mode	Vi Mode	Default Mode
bash	set -o emacs	set -o vi	emacs
ksh	set -o emacs	set -o vi	none
tcsh	bindkey -e	bindkey -v	emacs
zsh	bindkey -e	bindkey -v	emacs
zsh	set -o emacs	set -o vi	emacs

Emacs Mode

As you would expect, in emacs command line editing mode you can use the key bindings found in the emacs editor. For example, to move to the beginning of the command line type `Ctrl-a`. To recall the previous command type `Ctrl-p`.

`Esc Esc` - Escape completion. Similar to tab completion.

`Ctrl-b` - Move cursor to the left (back)

`Ctrl-f` - Move cursor to the right (forward)

`Ctrl-p` - Up (Previous command line)

`Ctrl-n` - Down (Next command line)

`Ctrl-e` - Move to the end of the line

`Ctrl-a` - Move to the beginning of the line

`Ctrl-x Ctrl-e` - Edit the current command line in the editor defined by the $EDITOR environment variable.

See the section in this book on the emacs editor for more key bindings.

Vi Mode

When you are using vi command line editing mode you start in insert mode so you can quickly type commands. To enter command mode, press `Esc`. To move to the previous command, for example, type `Esc` `k`. To resume editing enter insert mode by pressing `i`, `I`, `a`, or `A`.

`Esc` - Enter command mode.

Key bindings in command mode:

`\` - Vi style file completion. Similar to tab completion.

`h` - Move cursor left

`k` - Up (Previous command line)

`j` - Down (Next command line)

`l` - Move cursor right

`$` - Move to the end of the line

`^` - Move to the beginning of the line

`i` - Enter insert mode.

`a` - Enter insert mode, append text at current location.

A - Enter insert mode, append text at end of line.

I - Enter insert edit mode, prepend text to start of line.

v - Edit the current command line in the editor defined by the $EDITOR environment variable.

See the section in this book on the <u>vi editor</u> for more key bindings.

Dealing with Long Shell Commands

The backslash (\) is the line continuation character. You have learned how to use the backslash to escape special characters like spaces. However, when a backslash is placed at the end of a line it is used as a line continuation character. This allows you to create command lines that are displayed as multiple lines but are executed as a single command line by the shell. You can use line continuation to make commands more readable and easier to understand.

```
$ echo "one two three"
one two three
$ echo "one \
> two \
> three"
one two three
$ echo "onetwothree"
onetwothree
$ echo "one\
> two\
> three"
onetwothree
$
```

Notice the greater-than symbol (>) in the above example. It is the secondary prompt string and can be customized by changing the PS2 environment variable. You learned previously how to change the primary prompt string with PS1 in the "Customizing the Prompt" section of this book.

```
$ PS2="line continued: "
$ echo "one \
line continued: two \
line continued: three"
one two three
$
```

Environment Variables

You have already been introduced to environment variables and have put them to good use. To recap, an environment variable is a storage location that has a name and a value. They often effect the way programs behave. For example, you learned how to inform various programs about your preferred editor by defining the $EDITOR environment variable.

Common Environment Variables

Variable	Description
EDITOR	The program to run to perform edits.
HOME	The Home directory of the user.
LOGNAME	The login name of the user.
MAIL	The location of the user's local inbox.
OLDPWD	The previous working directory.
PATH	A colon separated list of directories to search for commands.
PAGER	This program may be called to view a file.

Variable	Description
PS1	The primary prompt string.
PWD	The present working directory.
USER	The username of the user.

Viewing Environment Variables

If you know the name of the environment variable that you want to examine, you can run `echo $VARIABLE_NAME` or `printenv VARIABLE_NAME`. If you want to examine all the environment variables that are set, use the `env` or `printenv` commands.

`printenv` - Print all or part of environment.

```
$ printenv HOME
/home/bob
$ echo $HOME
/home/bob
$ printenv
TERM=xterm-256color
SHELL=/bin/bash
USER=bob
PATH=/usr/local/bin:/usr/bin:/bin
MAIL=/var/mail/bob
PWD=/home/bob
LANG=en_US.UTF-8
HOME=/home/bob
LOGNAME=bob
$ env
TERM=xterm-256color
SHELL=/bin/bash
USER=bob
PATH=/usr/local/bin:/usr/bin:/bin
MAIL=/var/mail/bob
```

```
PWD=/home/bob
LANG=en_US.UTF-8
HOME=/home/bob
LOGNAME=bob
$
```

Exporting Environment Variables

When a process is started it inherits the exported environment variables of the process that spawned it. A variable that is set or changed only effects the current running process unless it is exported. The variables that are not exported are called local variables. The `export` command allows variables to be used by subsequently executed commands. Here is   an   example.

```
$ echo $PAGER

$ PAGER=less
$ echo $PAGER
less
$ bash
$ echo $PAGER

$ exit
exit
$ export PAGER=less
$ bash
$ echo $PAGER
less
$ exit
exit
$
```

In the above example PAGER was defined in the current environment. When you start a child process it inherits all the environment variables that were exported in your current environment. Since PAGER was not exported it was not set in the spawned bash shell. When you exported PAGER you saw that it was indeed available in the child process.

Removing Variables from the Environment

You can use `unset` to remove or delete an environment variable.

```
$ echo $PAGER
less
$ unset PAGER
$ echo $PAGER

$
```

Deep Dive

- Bash it - A framework for managing your bash configuration.
  https://github.com/revans/bash-it

- Command Line Completion - Tab completion explained.
  http://en.wikipedia.org/wiki/Command-line_completion

- Configuration Files for Shell - A list of files used to configure
  shell environments.
  http://en.wikipedia.org/wiki/Unix_shell#Configuration_files_for
  _shells

- Dotfiles.org - A place to upload, download, and share your
  dotfiles.
  http://dotfiles.org/

- Dotfiles.github.io - A guide to dotfiles on github.com.
  http://dotfiles.github.io/

- Oh my ZSH - A community-driven framework for managing your
  zsh configuration.
  https://github.com/robbyrussell/oh-my-zsh

- Shells

  - Bourne Shell
    https://en.wikipedia.org/wiki/Bourne_shell

  - Bash
    https://www.gnu.org/software/bash/

  - C Shell
    https://en.wikipedia.org/wiki/C_shell

  - Korn Shell
    http://www.kornshell.com/

  - tcsh
    http://www.tcsh.org/

  - Z Shell
    http://www.zsh.org/

- Using Bash History Interactively - Official Bash history documentation.
  http://www.gnu.org/software/bash/manual/bashref.html#Using-History-Interactively

- Unix Shell - An article on the shell user interface.
  https://en.wikipedia.org/wiki/Unix_shell

DAY 5

PROCESSES AND JOB CONTROL

Listing Processes and Displaying Information

To display the currently running processes use the ps command. If no options are specified, ps displays the processes associated with your current session. To see every process including ones that are not owned by you, use ps -e. To see processes running by a specific user, use ps -u username.

ps - Display process status.

Common ps options:

-e - Everything, all processes.

-f - Full format listing.

-u username - Display processes running as username.

-p pid - Display process information for pid. A PID is a process ID.

Common ps commands:

ps -e - Display all processes.

ps -ef - Display all processes.

ps -eH - Display a process tree.

ps -e --forest - Display a process tree.

ps -u username - Display processes running as username.

```
$ ps
  PID TTY          TIME CMD
19511 pts/2    00:00:00 bash
19554 pts/2    00:00:00 ps
$ ps -p 19511
  PID TTY          TIME CMD
19511 pts/2    00:00:00 bash
$ ps -f
UID         PID  PPID  C STIME TTY          TIME CMD
bob       19511 19509  0 16:50 pts/2    00:00:00 -bash
bob       19556 19511  0 16:50 pts/2    00:00:00 ps -f
$ ps -e | head
  PID TTY          TIME CMD
    1 ?        00:00:02 init
    2 ?        00:00:00 kthreadd
    3 ?        00:00:19 ksoftirqd/0
    5 ?        00:00:00 kworker/0:0H
    7 ?        00:00:00 migration/0
    8 ?        00:00:00 rcu_bh
    9 ?        00:00:17 rcu_sched
   10 ?        00:00:12 watchdog/0
   11 ?        00:00:00 khelper
$ ps -ef | head
UID         PID  PPID  C STIME TTY          TIME CMD
```

```
root              1     0  0 Dec27 ?     00:00:02 /sbin/init
root              2     0  0 Dec27 ?     00:00:00 [kthreadd]
root              3     2  0 Dec27 ?     00:00:19 [ksoftirqd/0]
root              5     2  0 Dec27 ?     00:00:00 [kworker/0:0H]
root              7     2  0 Dec27 ?     00:00:00 [migration/0]
root              8     2  0 Dec27 ?     00:00:00 [rcu_bh]
root              9     2  0 Dec27 ?     00:00:17 [rcu_sched]
root             10     2  0 Dec27 ?     00:00:12 [watchdog/0]
root             11     2  0 Dec27 ?     00:00:00 [khelper]
$ ps -fu www-data
UID         PID  PPID  C STIME TTY       TIME CMD
www-data    941   938  0 Dec27 ?     00:00:00
/usr/sbin/apache2 -k start
www-data    942   938  0 Dec27 ?     00:00:00
/usr/sbin/apache2 -k start
www-data    943   938  0 Dec27 ?     00:00:00
/usr/sbin/apache2 -k start
```

Here are other commands that allow you to view running processes.

pstree - Display running processes in a tree format.

htop - Interactive process viewer. This command is less common than top and may not be available on the system.

top - Interactive process viewer.

Running Processes in the Foreground and Background

Up until this point all the commands you have been executing have been running in the foreground. When a command, process, or program is running in the foreground the shell prompt will not be displayed until that process exits. For long running programs it can be convenient to send them to the background. Processes that are backgrounded still execute and perform their task, however they do not block you from entering further commands at the shell prompt. To background a process, place an ampersand (&) at the end of the command.

command & - **Start command in the background.**

Ctrl-c - **Kill the foreground process.**

Ctrl-z - **Suspend the foreground process.**

bg [%num] - **Background a suspended process.**

fg [%num] - **Foreground a background process.**

kill [%num] - **Kill a process by job number or PID.**

jobs [%num] - **List jobs.**

```
$ ./long-running-program &
[1] 22686
$ ps -p 22686
  PID TTY             TIME CMD
22686 pts/1     00:00:00 long-running-pr
$ jobs
[1]+  Running   ./long-running-program &
$ fg
./long-running-program
```

When a command is backgrounded two numbers are displayed. The number in brackets is the job number and can be referred by preceding it with the percent sign. The second number is the PID. Here is what it looks like to start multiple processes in the background.

```
$ ./long-running-program &
[1] 22703
$ ./long-running-program &
[2] 22705
$ ./long-running-program &
[3] 22707
$ ./long-running-program &
[4] 22709
```

```
$ jobs
[1]    Done           ./long-running-program
[2]    Done           ./long-running-program
[3]-   Running        ./long-running-program &
[4]+   Running        ./long-running-program &
```

The plus sign (+) in the `jobs` output represents the current job while the minus sign (–) represents the previous job. The current job is considered to be the last job that was stopped while it was in the foreground or the last job started in the background. The current job can be referred to by `%%` or `%+`. If no job information is supplied to the `fg` or `bg` commands, the current job is operated upon. The previous job can be referred to by `%–`.

You will notice that jobs number 1 and 2 are reported as being done. The shell does not interrupt your current command line, but will report job statuses right before a new prompt is displayed. For example, if you start a program in the background a prompt is returned. The shell will not report the status of the job until a new prompt is displayed. You can request a new prompt be displayed by simply hitting `Enter`.

To bring a job back to the foreground, type the name of the job or use the `fg` command. To foreground the current job execute `%%`, `%+`, `fg`, `fg %%`, `fg %+`, or **fg** `%num`. To foreground job number 3, execute `%3` or `fg %3`.

```
$ jobs
[3]-   Running        ./long-running-program &
[4]+   Running        ./long-running-program &
$ fg %3
./long-running-program
```

To pause or suspend a job that is running in the foreground, type `Ctrl-z`. Once a job is suspended it can be resumed in the foreground or background. To background a suspended job type the name of the job followed by an ampersand or use `bg` followed by the job name.

```
$ jobs
```

```
[1]    Running    ./long-running-program &
[2]-   Running    ./long-running-program &
[3]+   Running    ./another-program &
$ fg
./another-program
^Z
[3]+  Stopped    ./another-program
$ jobs
[1]    Running    ./long-running-program &
[2]-   Running    ./long-running-program &
[3]+  Stopped    ./another-program
$ bg %3
[3]+ ./another-program &
$ jobs
[1]    Running    ./long-running-program &
[2]-   Running    ./long-running-program &
[3]+   Running    ./another-program &
```

You can stop or kill a background job using the `kill` command. For example, to kill job number 1 execute `kill %1`. To kill a job that is running in the foreground, type `Ctrl-c`.

```
$ jobs
[1]    Running       ./long-running-program &
[2]-   Running       ./long-running-program &
[3]+   Running       ./another-program &
$ kill %1
[1]    Terminated    ./long-running-program
$ jobs
[2]-   Running       ./long-running-program &
[3]+   Running       ./another-program &
$ fg %2
./long-running-program
^C
$ jobs
[3]+   Running       ./another-program &
$
```

Killing Processes

Ctrl-c - Kills the foreground process.

kill [signal] pid - Send a signal to a process.

kill -l - Display a list of signals.

The default signal used by kill is termination. You will see this signal referred to as SIGTERM or TERM for short. Signals have numbers that correspond to their names. The default TERM signal is number 15. So running kill pid, kill -15 pid, and kill -TERM pid are all equivalent. If a process does not terminate when you send it the TERM signal, use the KILL signal which is number 9.

```
$ ps | grep hard-to-stop
27398 pts/1     00:00:00 hard-to-stop
$ kill 27398
$ ps | grep hard-to-stop
27398 pts/1     00:00:00 hard-to-stop
$ kill -9 27398
$ ps | grep hard-to-stop
$
```

Deep Dive

- Bash Documentation on Job Control
  http://gnu.org/software/bash/manual/html_node/Job-Control.html

SCHEDULING REPEATED JOBS WITH CRON

If you need to repeat a task on a schedule, you can use the cron service. Every minute the cron service checks to see if there are any scheduled jobs to run and if so runs them. Cron jobs are often used to automate a process or perform routine maintenance. You can schedule cron jobs by using the `crontab` command.

`cron` - A time based job scheduling service. This service is typically started when the system boots.

`crontab` - A program to create, read, update, and delete your job schedules.

A crontab (cron table) is a configuration file that specifies when commands are to be executed by cron. Each line in a crontab represents a job and contains two pieces of information: 1) when to run and 2) what to run. The time specification consists of five fields. They are minutes, hour, day of the month, month, and day of the week. After the time specification you provide the command to be executed.

Crontab Format

```
* * * * * command
| | | | |
| | | | +-- Day of the Week    (0-6)
| | | +---- Month of the Year  (1-12)
| | +------ Day of the Month   (1-31)
| +-------- Hour               (0-23)
+---------- Minute             (0-59)
```

The command will only be executed when all of the time specification fields match the current date and time. You can specify that a command be run only once, but this is not the typical use case for cron. Typically, one or more of the time specification fields will contain an asterisk (*) which matches any time or date for that field. Here is an example crontab.

```
# Run every Monday at 07:00.
0 7 * * 1 /opt/sales/bin/weekly-report
```

Here is a graphical representation of the above crontab entry.

```
0 7 * * 1 /opt/sales/bin/weekly-report
| | | | |
| | | | +-- Day of the Week    (0-6)
| | | +---- Month of the Year  (1-12)
| | +------ Day of the Month   (1-31)
| +-------- Hour               (0-23)
+---------- Minute             (0-59)
```

This job will run only when the minute is 0, the hour is 7, and the day of the week is 1. In the day of the week field 0 represents Sunday, 1 Monday, etc. This job will run on any day and during any month since the asterisk was used for those two fields.

If any output is generated by the command it is mailed to you. You can check your local mail with the mail command. If you would prefer not to get email you can redirect the output of the command as in this example.

```
# Run at 02:00 every day and send output to a log.
0 2 * * * /opt/acme/bin/backup > /tmp/backup.log 2>&1
```

You can provide multiple values for each of the fields. If you would like to run a command every half-hour, you could do this.

```
# Run every 30 minutes.
0,30 * * * * /opt/acme/bin/half-hour-check

# Another way to do the same thing.
*/2 * * * * /opt/acme/bin/half-hour-check
```

Instead of using 0,30 for the minute field you could have used */2. You can even use ranges with a dash. If you want to run a job every minute for the first four minutes of the hour you can use this time specification: 0-4 * * * * command.

There are several implementations of the cron scheduler and some allow you to use shortcuts and keywords in your crontabs. Common keywords have been provided below, but refer to the documentation for cron on your system to ensure these will work.

Keyword	Description	Equivalent
@yearly	Run once a year at midnight in the morning of January 1	0 0 1 1 *
@annually	Same as @yearly	0 0 1 1 *
@monthly	Run once a month at midnight in the morning of the first day of the month	0 0 1 * *
@weekly	Run once a week at midnight in the morning of Sunday	0 0 * * 0
@daily	Run once a day at midnight	0 0 * * *
@midnight	Same as @daily	0 0 * * *
@hourly	Run once an hour at the beginning of the hour	0 * * * *
@reboot	Run at startup	N/A

Using the Crontab Command

Use the `crontab` command to manipulate cron jobs.

`crontab file` - Install a new crontab from file.

`crontab -l` - List your cron jobs.

`crontab -e` - Edit your cron jobs.

`crontab -r` - Remove all of your cron jobs.

```
$ crontab -l
no crontab for bob
$ cat my-cron
# Run every Monday at 07:00.
0 7 * * 1 /opt/sales/bin/weekly-report
$ crontab my-cron
$ crontab -l
# Run every Monday at 07:00.
0 7 * * 1 /opt/sales/bin/weekly-report
$ crontab -e
# $EDITOR is invoked.
$ crontab -r
$ crontab -l
no crontab for bob
$
```

Deep Dive

- CronWFT - Decodes crontab lines. Print out human readable output.
  http://cronwtf.github.io/

- CronMaker - A utility which helps you to build cron expressions.
  http://www.cronmaker.com/

SWITCHING USERS AND RUNNING COMMANDS AS OTHERS

su

One way to start a session as another user on the system is to use the su command. If no arguments are supplied to su, it assumes you are trying to become the superuser. Executing su is the same as executing su root. Your current environment is passed to the new shell unless you specify a hyphen (-). In that case, su creates an environment like you would expect to see had you logged in as that user.

su [username] - Change user ID or become superuser

Common su options:

- - A hyphen is used to provide an environment similar to what the user would expect had the user logged in directly.

-c command - Specify a command to be executed. If the command is more than one word in length, it needs to be quoted.

```
bob@linuxsvr:~$ export TEST=1
bob@linuxsvr:~$ su oracle
Password:
oracle@linuxsvr:/home/bob$ echo $TEST
1
oracle@linuxsvr:/home/bob$ pwd
/home/bob
oracle@linuxsvr:/home/bob$ exit
exit
bob@linuxsvr:~$ su - oracle
Password:
oracle@linuxsvr:~$ echo $TEST

oracle@linuxsvr:~$ pwd
/home/oracle
oracle@linuxsvr:~$ exit
bob@linuxsvr:~$ su -c 'echo $ORACLE_HOME' oracle
Password:

bob@linuxsvr:~$ su -c 'echo $ORACLE_HOME' - oracle
Password:
/u01/app/oracle/product/current
bob@linuxsvr:~$
```

If you want to know what user you are working as, run the `whoami` command.

`whoami` - Displays the effective username.

```
$ whoami
bob
$ su oracle
Password:
$ whoami
oracle
$
```

Sudo - Super User Do

Another way to switch users or execute commands as others is to use the `sudo` command. Sudo allows you to run programs with the security privileges of another user. Like `su`, if no username is specified it assumes you are trying to run commands as the superuser. This is why sudo is referred to as super user do. It is commonly used to install, start, and stop applications that require superuser privileges.

`sudo` - Execute a command as another user, typically the superuser.

One advantage of using `sudo` over the `su` command is that you do not need to know the password of the other user. This can eliminate the issues that arise from using shared passwords and generic accounts. When you execute the `sudo` command you are prompted for your password. If the sudo configuration permits access, the command is executed. The sudo configuration is typically controlled by the system administrator and requires root access to change.

Using Sudo

Here are the common ways to use the `sudo` command.

`sudo -l` - List available commands.

`sudo command` - Run command as the superuser.

`sudo -u root command` - Same as **sudo command**.

`sudo -u user command` - Run command as user.

`sudo su` - Switch to the superuser account.

`sudo su -` - Switch to the superuser account with an environment like you would expect to see had you logged in as that user.

sudo su - username - Switch to the username account with an environment like you would expect to see had you logged in as that user.

```
$ sudo -l
User bob may run the following commands on this host:
(root) NOPASSWD: /etc/init.d/apache2
(fred) NOPASSWD: /opt/fredApp/bin/start
(fred) NOPASSWD: /opt/fredApp/bin/stop
(root) /bin/su - oracle
$ sudo /etc/init.d/apache2 start
 * Starting web server apache2
$ sudo -u fred /opt/fredApp/bin/start
Fred's app started as user fred.
$ sudo su - oracle
[sudo] password for bob:
oracle@linuxsvr:~$ whoami
oracle
oracle@linuxsvr:~$ exit
$ whoami
bob
$
```

The output of sudo -l displays what commands can be executed with sudo and under which account. In the above example, sudo will not prompt for a password for the commands preceded with NOPASSWD. This type of configuration may be required to automate jobs via cron that require escalated privileges.

Deep Dive

- The su command
  http://www.linfo.org/su.html

- Sudo - The official sudo website.
  http://www.sudo.ws/sudo/

- Ubuntu Sudo Documentation
  http://help.ubuntu.com/community/RootSudo

INSTALLING SOFTWARE

Typically when you install software on a Linux system you do so with a package. A package is a collection of files that make up an application. Additionally, a package contains data about the application as well as any steps required to successfully install and remove that application. The data, or metadata, that is contained within a package can include information such as the description of the application, the version of the application, and a list of other packages that it depends on. In order to install or remove a package you need to use superuser privileges.

A package manager is used to install, upgrade, and remove packages. Any additional software that is required for a package to function properly is known as a dependency. The package manager uses a package's metadata to automatically install the dependencies. Package managers keep track of what files belong to what packages, what packages are installed, and what versions of those packages are installed.

Installing Software on CentOS, Fedora, and RedHat Distributions

The yum command line utility is a package management program for Linux distributions that use the RPM package manager. CentOS, Fedora, Oracle Linux, RedHat Enterprise Linux, and Scientific Linux are RPM based distributions on which you can use yum.

yum search search-string - Search for search-string.

yum install [-y] package - Install package. Use the -y option to automatically answer yes to yum's questions.

yum remove package - Remove/uninstall package.

yum info [package] - Display information about package.

To search for software to install, use yum search search-string.

```
$ yum search inkscape
Loaded plugins: refresh-packagekit, security
============== N/S Matched: inkscape ==============
inkscape-docs.i686 : Documentation for Inkscape
inkscape.i686 : Vector-based drawing program using
SVG
inkscape-view.i686 : Viewing program for SVG files

  Name and summary matches only, use "search all" for
everything.
$
```

To install software, use yum install package. Installing software requires superuser privileges. This means you need to use sudo or switch to the root account with the su command.

```
$ sudo yum install inkscape
[sudo] password for bob:
```

```
Loaded plugins: refresh-packagekit, security
Setting up Install Process
Resolving Dependencies
--> Running transaction check
---> Package inkscape.i686 0:0.47-6.el6 will be
installed
--> Processing Dependency: python for package:
...
Dependencies Resolved
===========================================================
 Package     Arch   Version          Repository
Size
===========================================================
Installing:
 inkscape     i686   0.47-6.el6        base        8.6 M
Installing for dependencies:
 ImageMagick i686   6.5.4.7-7.el6_5   updates     1.7 M
...
Transaction Summary
===========================================================
Install     21 Package(s)

Total download size: 21 M
Installed size: 97 M
Is this ok [y/N]: y
Downloading Packages:
(1/21): ImageMagick-6.5.4.7-7.el6_5.i686.rpm
...
Installed:
  inkscape.i686 0:0.47-6.el6

Dependency Installed:
  ImageMagick.i686 0:6.5.4.7-7.el6_5
...
Complete!
```

To uninstall a package, use `yum remove`. Removing software requires superuser privileges.

```
$ sudo yum remove inkscape
Loaded plugins: refresh-packagekit, security
```

```
Setting up Remove Process
Resolving Dependencies
--> Running transaction check
---> Package inkscape.i686 0:0.47-6.el6 will be
erased
--> Finished Dependency Resolution

Dependencies Resolved

================================================================
 Package     Arch    Version        Repository        Size
================================================================
Removing:
 inkscape   i686    0.47-6.el6     @base             37 M

Transaction Summary
================================================================
Remove         1 Package(s)

Installed size: 37 M
Is this ok [y/N]: y
Downloading Packages:
Running rpm_check_debug
Running Transaction Test
Transaction Test Succeeded
Running Transaction
  Erasing    : inkscape-0.47-6.el6.i686    1/1
  Verifying  : inkscape-0.47-6.el6.i686    1/1

Removed:
  inkscape.i686 0:0.47-6.el6

Complete!
$
```

The rpm Command

In addition to the yum command, you can use the rpm command to interact with the package manager.

`rpm -qa` - List all the installed packages.

`rpm -qf /path/to/file` - List the package that contains file.

`rpm -ivh package.rpm` - Install a package from the file named package.rpm.

`rpm -ql package` - List all files that belong to package.

```
$ rpm -qa | sort | head
acl-2.2.49-6.el6.i686
acpid-1.0.10-2.1.el6.i686
aic94xx-firmware-30-2.el6.noarch
alsa-lib-1.0.22-3.el6.i686
alsa-plugins-pulseaudio-1.0.21-3.el6.i686
alsa-utils-1.0.22-5.el6.i686
anaconda-13.21.215-1.el6.centos.i686
anaconda-yum-plugins-1.0-5.1.el6.noarch
apache-tomcat-apis-0.1-1.el6.noarch
apr-1.3.9-5.el6_2.i686
$ rpm -qf /usr/bin/which
which-2.19-6.el6.i686
$ sudo rpm -ivh SpiderOak-5.0.3-1.i386.rpm
[sudo] password for bob:
Preparing...          ##################### [100%]
   1:SpiderOak        ##################### [100%]
$
```

Installing Software on Debian and Ubuntu

The Debian and Ubuntu distributions use a package manager called APT, the Advanced Packaging Tool. APT is comprised of a few small utilities with the two most commonly used ones being `apt-cache` and `apt-get`.

`apt-cache search search-string` - Search for search-string.

`apt-get install [-y] package` - Install package. Use the `-y` option to automatically answer yes to apt-get's questions.

`apt-get remove package` - **Remove/uninstall package,** leaving behind configuration files.

`apt-get purge package` - **Remove/uninstall package,** deleting configuration files.

`apt-cache show package` - **Display information about package.**

To search for software to install, use `apt-cache search search-string.`

```
$ apt-cache search inkscape
create-resources - shared resources for use by
creative applications
inkscape - vector-based drawing program
python-scour - SVG scrubber and optimizer
fonts-opendin - Open DIN font
fonts-rufscript - handwriting-based font for Latin
characters
ink-generator - Inkscape extension to automatically
generate files from a template
lyx - document processor
robocut - Control program for Graphtec cutting
plotters
sozi - inkscape extension for creating animated
presentations
ttf-rufscript - handwriting-based font for Latin
characters (transitional dummy package)
$
```

To install software, use `apt-get install package.` **Installing software requires superuser privileges. This means you need to use** `sudo` **or switch to the root account with the** `su` **command.**

```
$ sudo apt-get install inkscape
Reading package lists... Done
Building dependency tree
Reading state information... Done
The following extra packages will be installed:
  aspell aspell-en cmap-adobe-japan1 dbus-x11
```

```
...
3 upgraded, 74 newly installed, 0 to remove and 96
not upgraded.
Need to get 62.7 MB of archives.
After this operation, 171 MB of additional disk space
will be used.
Do you want to continue [Y/n]? y
...
Setting up perlmagick (8:6.6.9.7-5ubuntu3.2) ...
Processing triggers for libc-bin ...
ldconfig deferred processing now taking place
$
```

To uninstall a package, use `apt-get` remove. **Removing software requires superuser privileges.**

```
$ sudo apt-get remove inkscape
Reading package lists... Done
Building dependency tree
Reading state information... Done
The following packages will be REMOVED:
  inkscape
0 upgraded, 0 newly installed, 1 to remove and 96 not
upgraded.
After this operation, 64.9 MB disk space will be
freed.
Do you want to continue [Y/n]? y
(Reading database ... 69841 files and directories
currently installed.)
Removing inkscape ...
Processing triggers for man-db ...
Processing triggers for hicolor-icon-theme ...
$
```

The dpkg Command

In addition the `apt` utilities, you can use the `dpkg` command to interact with the package manager.

`dgpk -1` - List all the installed packages.

`dpkg -S /path/to/file` - List the package that contains file.

`dpkg -i package.deb` - Install a package from the file named package.deb.

`dpkg -L package` - List all files that belong to package.

```
$ dpkg -l | head
Desired=Unknown/Install/Remove/Purge/Hold
| Status=Not/Inst/Conf-files/Unpacked/halF-conf/Half-
inst/trig-aWait/Trig-pend
|/ Err?=(none)/Reinst-required (Status,Err:
uppercase=bad)
||/ Name              Version
Description
+++-==================-=============-===================
ii  accountsservice  0.6.15-2ubuntu9.6      query
and manipulate user account information
ii  acpid            1:2.0.10-1ubuntu3      Advanced
Configuration and Power Interface event daemon
ii  adduser          3.113ubuntu2           add and
remove users and groups
ii  apparmor         2.7.102-0ubuntu3.9     User-
space parser utility for AppArmor
ii  apport           2.0.1-0ubuntu17.5
automatically generate crash reports for debugging
$ dpkg -S /usr/bin/which
debianutils: /usr/bin/which
$ sudo dpkg -i spideroak_5.1.3_i386.deb
[sudo] password for bob:
Selecting previously unselected package spideroak.
(Reading database ... 153942 files and directories
currently installed.)
Unpacking spideroak (from spideroak_5.1.3_i386.deb)
...
Setting up spideroak (1:5.1.3) ...
Processing triggers for man-db ...
Processing triggers for desktop-file-utils ...
Processing triggers for bamfdaemon ...
```

```
Rebuilding /usr/share/applications/bamf.index...
Processing triggers for gnome-menus ...
$
```

Free Video on Installing Linux Software

If you would like to see exactly what it's like to install software on a Linux system, check out this video that I put together for you: http://www.linuxtrainingacademy.com/installing/

Deep Dive

- Managing Software with Yum
  https://www.centos.org/docs/5/html/yum/

- AptGet Howto
  https://help.ubuntu.com/community/AptGet/Howto

- Ubuntu - Installing Software
  https://help.ubuntu.com/community/InstallingSoftware

- Installing Linux Software Video
  http://www.linuxtrainingacademy.com/installing/

THE END AND THE BEGINNING

Even though this is the end of this book, I sincerely hope that it is just the beginning of your Linux journey. Linux has been growing steadily in popularity since its release in 1991. You will find Linux running on phones, laptops, servers, supercomputers, industrial equipment, and even on medical devices. The possibilities for learning, exploring, and growing are endless.

ABOUT THE AUTHOR

Jason Cannon started his career as a Unix and Linux System Engineer in 1999. Since that time he has utilized his Linux skills at companies such as Xerox, UPS, Hewlett-Packard, and Amazon.com. Additionally, he has acted as a technical consultant and independent contractor for small to medium businesses.

Jason has professional experience with CentOS, RedHat Enterprise Linux, SUSE Linux Enterprise Server, and Ubuntu. He has used several Linux distributions on personal projects including Debian, Slackware, CrunchBang, and others. In addition to Linux, Jason has experience supporting proprietary Unix operating systems including AIX, HP-UX, and Solaris.

He enjoys teaching others how to use and exploit the power of the Linux operating system and teaches online video training courses at http://www.LinuxTrainingAcademy.com.

Jason is also the author of *Python Programming for Beginners* and *Command Line Kung Fu: Bash Scripting Tricks, Linux Shell ProgrammingTips, and Bash One-Liners*

OTHER BOOKS BY THE AUTHOR

Bash Command Line Pro Tips
http://www.linuxtrainingacademy.com/bash-pro-tips

Command Line Kung Fu: Bash Scripting Tricks, Linux Shell Programming
Tips, and Bash One-liners
http://www.linuxtrainingacademy.com/command-line-kung-fu-book

High Availability for the LAMP Stack: Eliminate Single Points of Failure
and Increase Uptime for Your Linux, Apache, MySQL, and PHP Based
Web Applications
http://www.linuxtrainingacademy.com/ha-lamp-book

Python Programming for Beginners
http://www.linuxtrainingacademy.com/python-programming-for-
beginners

ADDITIONAL RESOURCES INCLUDING EXCLUSIVE DISCOUNTS FOR YOU

For even more resources, visit:
http://www.linuxtrainingacademy.com/resources

Books

Command Line Kung Fu
http://www.linuxtrainingacademy.com/command-line-kung-fu-book

Do you think you have to lock yourself in a basement reading cryptic man pages for months on end in order to have ninja like command line skills? In reality, if you had someone share their most powerful command line tips, tricks, and patterns you'd save yourself a lot of time and frustration. This book does just that.

High Availability for the LAMP Stack
http://www.linuxtrainingacademy.com/ha-lamp-book

Eliminate Single Points of Failure and Increase Uptime for Your Linux, Apache, MySQL, and PHP Based Web Applications

Python Programming for Beginners
http://www.linuxtrainingacademy.com/python-programming-for-beginners

If you are interested in learning how to program, or Python specifically, this book is for you. In it you will learn how to install Python, which version to choose, how to prepare your computer for a great experience, and all the computer programming basics you'll need to know to start writing fully functional programs.

Scrum Essentials
http://www.linuxtrainingacademy.com/scrum-book

This book will provide every team member, manager, and executive with a common understanding of Scrum, a shared vocabulary they can use in applying it, and practical knowledge for deriving maximum value from it. After reading Scrum Essentials you will know about scrum roles, sprints, scrum artifacts, and much more.

Courses

High Availability for the LAMP Stack
http://www.linuxtrainingacademy.com/ha-lamp-stack

Learn how to setup a highly available LAMP stack (Linux, Apache, MySQL, PHP). You'll learn about load balancing, clustering databases, creating distributed file systems, and more.

Linux for Beginners
http://www.linuxtrainingacademy.com/lfb-udemy

This is the online video training course based on this book. This course includes explanations as well as real-world examples on actual Linux systems.

Learn Linux in 5 Days
http://www.linuxtrainingacademy.com/linux-in-5-days

Take just 45 minutes a day for the next 5 days and I will teach you exactly what you need to know about the Linux operating system. You'll learn the most important concepts and commands, and I'll even guide you step-by-step through several practical and real-world examples.

Linux Alternatives to Windows Applications
http://www.linuxtrainingacademy.com/linux-alternatives

If you ever wanted to try Linux, but were afraid you wouldn't be able to use your favorite software, programs, or applications, take this course.

LPI Level 1 / Exam 101 Training
http://www.linuxtrainingacademy.com/lpi-course-1

This course provides interactive step-by-step videos that will help you prepare for the LPIC-1 101 Exam. This exam is important to help you prepare for the Linux+ and LPIC level 1 certification and this course provides all the materials you need to pass the exam.

LPI Level 1 / Exam 102 Training
http://www.linuxtrainingacademy.com/lpi-course-2

This course provides interactive, step-by-step videos that will help you prepare for the LPIC-1 102 Exam. This exam is important to help you prepare for the Linux+ and LPIC level 1 certification and this course provides all the materials you need to pass the exam.

Python for Beginners
http://www.linuxtrainingacademy.com/python-video-course

This comprehensive course covers the basics of Python as well as the more advanced aspects such as debugging and handling files. Enroll in this course to gain access to all 13 chapters of this Python for Beginners course as well as labs and code files.

Cloud Hosting and VPS (Virtual Private Servers)

Digital Ocean
http://www.linuxtrainingacademy.com/digitalocean

Simple cloud hosting, built for developers. Deploy an SSD cloud server in just 55 seconds. You can have your own server for as little as $5 a month.

Web Hosting with SSH and Shell Access

Bluehost
http://www.linuxtrainingacademy.com/bluehost

99% of my websites are hosted on Bluehost. Why? Because it's incredibly easy to use with 1-click automatic WordPress installation and excellent customer service - via phone and via chat. I HIGHLY RECOMMEND using Bluehost for your first site. Also, you can use the same hosting account for multiple domains if you plan on creating more websites. Visit http://www.linuxtrainingacademy.com/bluehost to get a special discount off the regular price!

HostGator
http://www.linuxtrainingacademy.com/hostgator

If you want an alternative to Bluehost, check out HostGator. It comes with a 99.9% uptime guarantee and includes a free site builder. They provide customer support 24 hours a day, seven days a week and even provide a 45 day money-back gaurantee..

APPENDICES

APPENDIX A:

ABBREVIATIONS AND ACRONYMS

ACL - access control list

APT - advanced packaging tool (apt)

ASCII - American Standard Code for Information Interchange

CentOS - Community ENTerprise Operating System

cd - Change directory

CLI - command line interface

crontab - cron table

dir - directory

distro - Distribution, a collection of user programs, software, and the Linux kernel to create an operating environment.

FOSS - free open source software

FTP - file transfer protocol

GID - group identification

GB - gigabyte

GNU - GNU's Not UNIX. (See GNU.org)

GUI - graphical user interface

HP - Hewlett-Packard

IBM - International Business Machines

KB - kilobyte

I/O - input/output

LFS - Linux from scratch.
(See http://www.linuxfromscratch.org/)

LSB - Linux Standard Base

LUG - Linux user group

LVM - logical volume management

MB - megabyte

MBR - master boot record

NFS - network file system

NTP - network time protocol

OS - operating system

PID - process identification number

POSIX - portable operating system interface

pwd - present working directory

RHEL - RedHat Enterprise Linux

RHCE - Red Hat Certified Engineer

RPM - RedHat Package Manager

SAN - storage area network

SELinux - Security Enhanced Linux

SFTP - secure file transfer protocol or SSH file transfer protocol

SGID - set group ID

SLES - SuSE Linux Enterprise Server

SSH - secure shell

STDIN - Standard input

STDOUT - Standard output

STDERR - Standard error

su - superuser

sudo - superuser do

SUID - set user ID

symlink - symbolic link

tar - tape archive

TB - terabyte

TTY - teletype terminal

UID - user identification

VDI - virtual disk image

X - X window system

YUM - Yellowdog Updater, Modified (yum)

APPENDIX B: FAQ

Q: Where can I access all the links in this book?

The links covered in this book along with other supplemental material is available at:

http://www.linuxtrainingacademy.com/lfb

Q: What is Linux?

Linux is an open-source operating system modelled after UNIX.

Q: What is the Linux kernel?

The Linux kernel handles the interactions between the software running on the system and the hardware. To learn more, visit the official Linux kernel website at http://www.kernel.org.

Q: Which Linux distribution should I use?

If your goal is to eventually become a Linux system administrator, focus on CentOS or Ubuntu. CentOS is a Red Hat Enterprise Linux (RHEL) derivative. As a general rule, CentOS and RHEL are often found in corporate environments. Ubuntu is popular with startups and smaller companies that run their operations in the cloud. If you are using Linux for your own personal reasons, choose a distribution that appeals to you. To get some ideas look at DistroWatch.com's top 10 distributions page.

Here are some other common Linux distributions:

- Arch Linux - https://www.archlinux.org/

- Debian - http://www.debian.org/

- Fedora - http://fedoraproject.org/

- LinuxMint - http://www.linuxmint.com/

- Mageia - http://www.mageia.org/

- openSUSE - http://www.opensuse.org/

There are several special purpose Linux distributions that focus on a single area. Examples areas of focus include education, minimalism, multimedia, networking/firewalls, and security. Here is just a sampling of the available specialty distros.

- ArtistX - A DVD which turns a computer into a full multimedia production studio.
  http://artistx.org/

- Edubuntu - An education oriented operating system.
  http://www.edubuntu.com/

- live.linuX-gamers.net - A live Linux distribution focused on gaming.
  http://live.linux-gamers.net/

- Mythbuntu - Mythbuntu is focused upon setting up a

standalone MythTV based PVR (personal video recorder) system.
http://www.mythbuntu.org/

- Parted Magic - A Hard disk management solution. https://partedmagic.com/

- Scientific Linux - Scientific Linux is put together by Fermilab, CERN, and various other labs and universities around the world. Its primary purpose is to reduce duplicated effort of the labs, and to have a common install base for the various experimenters.
https://www.scientificlinux.org/

- Ubuntu Studio - Provides the full range of multimedia content creation applications for audio, graphics, video, photography and publishing.
http://ubuntustudio.org/

- VortexBox - VortexBox is a multifunctional solution to rip, store and stream CDs, digital music and Internet radio. http://www.vortexbox.co.uk/

Q: Can I use Microsoft Office in Linux?

Microsoft Office is not available for Linux, however there are alternatives such as Libreoffice, Open Office, and AbiWord.

Q: How do I run XYZ program in Linux?

To find Linux alternatives for software you use on Mac and Windows, visit http://alternativeto.net/.

APPENDIX C: TRADEMARKS

BSD/OS is a trademark of Berkeley Software Design, Inc. in the United States and other countries.

Facebook is a registered trademark of Facebook, Inc..

Firefox is a registered trademark of the Mozilla Foundation.

HP and HEWLETT-PACKARD are registered trademarks that belong to Hewlett-Packard Development Company, L.P.

IBM® is a registered trademark of International Business Machines Corp., registered in many jurisdictions worldwide.

Linux® is the registered trademark of Linus Torvalds in the U.S. and other countries.

Mac and OS X are trademarks of Apple Inc., registered in the U.S. and other countries.

Open Source is a registered certification mark of Open Source Initiative.

Sun and Oracle Solaris are trademarks or registered trademarks of Oracle Corporatoin and/or its affiliates in the United States and other countries.

UNIX is a registered trademark of The Open Group.

Windows is a registered trademark of Microsoft Corporation in the United States and other countries.

All other product names mentioned herein are the trademarks of their respective owners.